From
Triumphalism
to Maturity

DONALD A. CARSON

From Triumphalism to Maturity

An Exposition of 2 Corinthians 10-13

Baker Book House
Grand Rapids, Michigan 49506

To
Pete and Gail Golz

Contents

Preface

I love the apostle Paul. Some people cannot understand my love. They find Paul angular, merely intellectual, intimidating, even arrogant. My response, firmly stated, is that they do not know him.

Despite my love for Paul, I have written very little about him. For one reason or another, my attention during the past dozen years has largely been devoted to Matthew and John, or to broader New Testament themes. Nevertheless I have taught the Pauline corpus to successive generations of seminary students and preached through several of his epistles to various congregations. Preparing for such assignments has gradually exposed me to substantial parts of the vast literature that has grown up around the Acts of the Apostles and the epistles of Paul. I do not claim to have mastered all of that literature, but I have come to know Paul a little better. And truly to know him is to love him.

Arguably, the most intense chapters in all of his writings are those studied here, viz., 2 Corinthians 10-13. Certainly they reveal more about Paul himself—his sufferings, values, motives, wrestlings, and self-perceptions—than any other four chapters of comparable length; yet far from promoting egocentricity, they point unerringly to Jesus Christ and to what it means to be a Christian. Moreover, this short part of Scripture speaks volumes to the modern church, especially in the West; so I resolved with God's help to devote the next volume in this series to these chapters.

Most of the material in this book has been the stuff of sermons in churches and conferences in Canada, America, and England. It has been worked over afresh for the printed page; but I have retained the movement from exegesis to application that serves as one of the markers distinguishing sermon from lecture. My hope is that this will encourage Christians, not only to read the Bible in its own historical and theological context, but to apply it with sensitivity and discernment to their own lives and to the modern church. I hope as well that some readers will come to love Paul as I do. There is little danger that such love would ever prove idolatrous; for to know Paul is to learn he puts "no stumbling block in anyone's path" (2 Cor 6:3) and to discover that imitating him points us away from him to imitating the Lord Jesus Christ (1 Cor 11:1). If that is what we begin to learn, Paul himself would be overjoyed.

I am very grateful to Marty Irwin for her customary skill and courtesy in transforming my manuscript into the millions of electrical blips the computer understands, and thus preparing the work for publication.

Soli Deo gloria.

D. A. Carson
Trinity Evangelical Divinity School

This is not a technical commentary, and so I have avoided the detailed references of that genre. When the two earlier volumes in the series were published, however, several readers suggested I might provide a list of English commentaries. I have adopted that suggestion, and have occasionally quoted choice passages from them, identifying the work by the author's name only. By and large I have avoided explicit reference to foreign-language works, journal articles, and the like, even though I have frequently interacted with their substance. There were two foreign-language commentaries I could not bring myself to eliminate from the following list of cited sources.

E. B. Allo. *Saint Paul: Seconde Epitre aux Corinthiens.* Paris: Gabalda, 1956.
C. K. Barrett. *The Second Epistle to the Corinthians.* London: Black, 1973.
J. A. Beet. *II Corinthians.* London: Hodder and Stoughton, 1982.
J. A. Bengel. *Gnomon of the New Testament.* Vol. 3. Edinburgh: T and T Clark, 1857.
F. F. Bruce. *1 and 2 Corinthians.* London: Oliphants, 1971.
John Calvin. *II Corinthians—Philemon.* Edinburgh: Oliver and Boyd, 1964.
James Denney. *II Corinthians.* London: Hodder and Stoughton, 1894.
A. R. Fausset. "II Corinthians," *Commentary on the Bible.* London: Collins, 1874.
H. L. Goudge. *II Corinthians.* London: Methuen, 1927.
M. J. Harris, "2 Corinthians," *The Expositor's Bible Commentary.* Vol. 10. Grand Rapids: Zondervan, 1976.

Matthew Henry. *Commentary on the Whole Bible*. London: Fisher, 1845.

Charles Hodge. *II Corinthians*. London: Banner of Truth, 1959.

Philip E. Hughes. *Paul's Second Epistle to the Corinthians*. Grand Rapids: Eerdmans, 1962.

H. Lietzmann. *An die Korinther I,II*. Tuebingen: J. C. B. Mohr, 1969. (Supplemented by W. G. Kuemmel).

Allan Mengies. *II Corinthians*. London: Macmillan, 1912.

H. A. W. Meyer. *Critical and Exegetical Handbook to the Epistles to the Corinthians*. Edinburgh: T and T Clark, 1964.

A. Robertson and A. Plummer. *II Corinthians*. Edinburgh: T and T Clark, 1915.

J. Waite. *II Corinthians*. London: John Murray, 1881.

Geoffrey Wilson. *2 Corinthians: A Digest of Reformed Comment*. Edinburgh: Banner of Truth, 1973.

1

Orientation to
2 Corinthians 10-13

We increasingly inhabit a time and place in Western history when humility is perceived to be a sign of weakness; when meekness is taken for a vice, not a virtue; when puff is more important than substance; when leadership, even in the church, frequently has more to do with politics, pizzazz, and showmanship, or with structure and hierarchy, than with spiritual maturity and conformity to Jesus Christ; when the budget is thought to be a more important indicator of ecclesiastical success than prayerfulness; and when loose talk of spiritual experience wins an instant following, even when that talk is mingled with a scarcely concealed haughtiness that has learned neither humility nor tears. To Christians hungry to understand and repent of these evils, 2 Corinthians 10-13 speaks with rare power and passion.

These chapters are among the most emotionally intense of all that the apostle Paul wrote. Partly for that reason, they are also among the most difficult. His language is frequently passionate, his rhetorical questions emotive, his sequence of thought compressed, his syntax broken (as a glance at the various translations of, say, 2 Cor 13:2 readily suggests!). Wisdom therefore dictates that we scout the text ahead of us; and that is the purpose of this chapter. Some readers may prefer to skip immediately to chapter 2, but a reading of the exposition without adequate knowledge of the background may prove unnecessarily frustrating.

1

We raise two questions:

A. Why Focus on 2 Corinthians 10-13?

1. Because these chapters most clearly reveal the heart and mind of the apostle Paul. More generally, of course, we could say it is important to study these chapters just because they constitute part of the Word of God; and it is difficult to imagine that someone who has taken the first steps toward loving God with heart and soul and mind and strength (Mark 12:30) would not want to absorb as much of God's Word as possible. In addition, of course, these chapters contain several well-known passages that have provided comfort and encouragement to countless generations of Christians. The "thorn in the flesh" passage (2 Cor 12:1-10) springs to mind most insistently, with its startling promise, "My grace is sufficient for you, for my power is made perfect in weakness" (12:9)—a promise heralded in many a hymn and chorus. But there are of course many other parts of Scripture to learn, and each has its own collection of gems. What makes this passage unique is the clarity with which it reveals the heart and mind of the apostle Paul.

This is no small gain, and our joy in finding it cannot be ridiculed as the historian's delight in antiquarian detail. Whether one acknowledges it or not, a great deal of what we learn comes by imitating someone else. For that reason Paul does not hesitate to tell his converts to imitate him, inasmuch as he imitates Christ (1 Cor 4:16; 11:1; 1 Thess 1:6; cf. Eph 5:1; 1 Thess 2:14; Heb 6:12). Close to the heart of the business of discipling another in the Christian faith is the self-discipline of serving as a model to the apprentice. Actions do not necessarily speak more loudly than words; but they usually do. In 2 Corinthians 10-13 we can see at a distance of nearly two thousand years, not only what Paul taught, but also how he lived; and his example still helps thoughtful Christians to live in greater conformity to the supreme pattern, the Lord Jesus himself.

At a superficial level, we learn from these chapters far more about Paul's sufferings than we do from the book of Acts. Luke tells us of one shipwreck; Paul informs us (2 Cor 11:25) of three others that took place before the one mentioned in Acts. Luke never mentions the Jewish floggings Paul received; Paul enumerates five such beatings (v. 24). Luke rather dryly narrates Paul's escape from Damascus (Acts 9:23-25), apparently seeing in the event something of God's gracious providence; Paul looks back on the same experience with a profound sense of shame (2 Cor 11:30-33). Yet these and other bits of information are not superficial after all, for they enable us to appreciate a side of apostleship we are prone to overlook: its immense capacity to suffer for Jesus' sake.

That prompts us to consider the second feature of Paul's life brought to sharp focus here—his style of leadership, the manner in which he exercised his apostolic authority. Here is a Paul who can threaten (2 Cor 13:2), explain (12:10), love (11:11), rebuke (12:11), and even use sarcasm (v. 16). But when? And why? Are such apostolic tools reflections of a lordly authority, or of a servant of Christ who is reluctant to use the full power with which God has equipped him? In what sense does Paul stand as a normative example for Christian leadership today?

Certainly another area worthy of the most scrupulous emulation is Paul's handling of boasting. This is so central a theme here that we shall return to it repeatedly. For now it is sufficient to say that Paul is normally very reticent to speak about the wonderful things God performs through him or reveals to him. His axiom is, "Let him who boasts, boast in the Lord" (2 Cor 10:17). Nevertheless, in these chapters we find Paul boasting, even though he is intensely embarrassed to be forced into such talk (e.g., 11:16-18). What prompts him to take these steps? In what ways does modern Christian self-promotion emulate Paul in this matter, and in what ways do we diverge from him?

Finally, Paul warns the Corinthian church about the dangers of false leadership. If the Corinthians could be deceived by people whom Paul characterizes as "false apostles, deceitful workmen, masquerading as apostles of Christ" (2 Cor 11:13), may we not be similarly deceived? What perspectives will preserve us from this danger? How should we apply to ourselves (as Paul applied to the Corinthians) his frightening demand, "Examine yourselves to see whether you are in the faith; test yourselves" (13:5)?

Knitting together all these concerns, yet going beyond them, is the apostolic example as a man under fire. Perhaps one of the most difficult charges a mature Christian leader may face is the double-barreled barb that he lacks credentials and effectiveness while exercising too much authority. The charge, of course, may in some cases be valid; but if not, it is notoriously difficult to answer. If a leader replies to the first part of the criticism by listing his credentials and service, his critics may respond by leaning on the second: "Ah, see, didn't we tell you? He is so arrogant he keeps talking about himself." If, on the other hand, the leader downplays his significance in order to disprove the charge of arrogance, his critics may always reply, "There's the problem; he has no real leadership potential." With just such a combination Paul is charged, only in his case the array of accusations is even more complex. His letters, his opponents say, are weighty, although in person he amounts to little (2 Cor 10:10). How then shall Paul respond by letter? If he says little, he will not be able to tackle the nest of problems; if he says much, his strong letter will be readily dismissed as typical. He is charged with being an inferior apostle (11:5); but if he lists his credentials, he will find himself boasting on the grounds of unhealthy comparisons between himself and others—a practice he condemns (10:12). He is accused of not being willing to receive support from the Corinthian church (11:7-8)—and is also charged with surreptitiously diverting funds gathered for Christians in Jerusalem to line his own pockets (see comments on 12:16).

Probably Paul would not even have bothered to answer these and other charges had not the gospel itself been at stake. The interlopers who were leading the Corinthian church astray were not only personally ambitious, they were preaching what Paul discerned to be a false gospel, another Jesus (2 Cor 11:4). That left Paul no alternative but to enter the fray; and the way he does this, with wisdom, wit, humor, irony, winsomeness, yet also anguish, hurt, and stunning emotional intensity, constitutes a marvellous case study in Christian leadership and the main-tenance of Christian values and priorities.

These chapters merit close scrutiny not only because they clearly reveal the heart and mind of the apostle Paul, but also:

2. Because they constitute a unit of thought (such as the Sermon on the Mount [Matt 5-7], e.g., or the Olivet discourse [Matt 24-25; Mark 13; Luke 21]).

Perhaps the easiest way to see this is to set 2 Corinthians

10-13 against the background of Paul's dealings and correspondence with the Corinthian church. According to Acts 18, Paul first
preached the gospel in Corinth during his second missionary
journey. He began by supporting himself with his trade while
living at the home of Aquila and Priscilla, who had recently
moved to Corinth from Rome (vv. 1-3). As usual, Paul opened
his ministry by attempting to win over to Jesus Messiah all those
who, Jews and Gentiles, frequented the synagogue (v. 4). Paul's
ministry multiplied when Silas and Timothy, who had been
discharging various responsibilities in Macedonia, rejoined him;
for either they took over the task of earning enough money for
the team to pay its way, or, more likely, they brought with them
enough money donated by the recently planted churches in
Macedonia to enable Paul to devote himself exclusively to
preaching (v. 5). Multiplied ministry was accompanied by
multiplied opposition; and so once again Paul was forced to
abandon his synagogue ministry and focus his attention on the
Gentiles. Paul moved his base of operations next door to the
house of Titius Justus (v. 7); and his ministry was so successful
that not only did many pagan Corinthians believe the gospel and
seek baptism, but Crispus himself, the synagogue ruler, along
with his entire household, believed in the Lord Jesus (v. 8).

Battered by repeated attacks, only recently delivered from
bruising punishment in Philippi (Acts 16), and having just barely
escaped the tender mercies of a mob in Berea (17:13-15), Paul
succumbed to fear and discouragement. The exalted Christ
spoke to Paul in a vision one night, and offered words of
encouragement and an incentive to persevere: "Do not be afraid;
keep on speaking, do not be silent. For I am with you, and no
one is going to attack and harm you, because I have many
people in this city" (18:9-10). Of course, the many people Christ
already "had" were not yet Christians; but the Lord's gracious
election here serves as a marvelous incentive to evangelism and
to a persevering proclamation of the gospel. At any rate, Paul
stayed a year and a half, saw the church well established, and
taught them the word of God (v. 11). In the spring of (probably)
A.D. 52, Paul left Corinth by ship: he crossed the Aegean Sea
with Priscilla and Aquila and arrived at Ephesus. On this
occasion, Paul did not stay long. He left Priscilla and Aquila
there, and headed for Jerusalem at a fast pace, hoping to arrive

for the feast (Passover or Pentecost). After a short stay in Jerusalem, Paul traveled north to Antioch in Syria, his "home church," resuming fellowship and friendship with many friends, and then returned to Ephesus. Thus began the two-and-a-half year ministry of enormous fruitfulness at Ephesus (probably fall of A.D. 52 to spring of A.D. 55), and it was during this period that the Corinthian correspondence was composed.

At some point (we do not know exactly when) Paul sent his Corinthian converts a letter, now lost, which we may designate Corinthians A. Paul refers to that early letter in 1 Corinthians 5:9-11, where the context makes it clear Paul is distinguishing between Corinthians A and our 1 Corinthians (which thus becomes Corinthians B, in order of sequence). In the former, he warned his converts against fornication and other vices, telling them to dissociate themselves from those who practice such things; but now in 1 Corinthians, he further explains that he did not mean by this prohibition to enforce a total separation between Christians and "the people of this world who are immoral, or the greedy and swindlers, or idolators. In that case you would have to leave this world." Rather, he explains, he was telling them in the first letter that they "must not associate with anyone *who calls himself a brother* but is sexually immoral or greedy, an idolator or a slanderer, a drunkard or a swindler. With such a man," Paul adds, "do not even eat." In other words, Paul was demanding church discipline, even excommunication if necessary, not the complete withdrawal of a severe hermitage.

There were broader reasons why, sometime during his Ephesian ministry, Paul wrote 1 Corinthians. Paul had received verbal reports from "some from Chloe's household" (1 Cor 1:11) of factionalism within the Corinthian church; and this ugly divisiveness was allied with arrogance (which is always a threat to the power of the gospel). Mutual resentments ended up in personal lawsuits, and even toleration for gross sexual promiscuity. On top of all that, three men, Stephanas, Fortunatus, and Achaicus (16:17) were sent as official delegates of the Corinthian church; and along with gifts, they (apparently) brought a letter (cf. 7:1) from the church asking a series of questions about marriage, sex, eating meat that had been offered to idols, the necessary characteristics of an apostle, the Lord's Supper, tongues, the nature of our bodies at the resurrection, and much more. Paul's extended answer to oral reports and written questions alike is our 1 Corinthians.

When Paul sent this letter off, he fully expected to follow it up with a personal visit. He intended to stay at Ephesus until the feast of Pentecost (probably A.D. 54 or 55; cf. 1 Cor 16:8), then cross the Aegean Sea to Macedonia to visit the churches he had planted there, and continue his journey south to Corinth, where, he promised, he would remain "awhile, or even spend the winter" (vv. 5,6). In the meantime, he sent Timothy and insisted the Corinthians should receive him warmly and "send him on his way in peace" (vv. 10-11; cf. Acts 19:22), so that he could return to Paul, presumably bearing a report. Shortly after sending off 1 Corinthians, however, Paul changed his plan a little: he proposed to visit the Corinthians twice, once on his way to Macedonia, and a second time on his way back; and from there he intended to sail for Judea (2 Cor 1:15,16), along with considerable money and several delegates of churches contributing these funds to the relief of the Jerusalem church, still suffering from famine and persecution.

Unfortunately, these happy plans had to be modified again. They were all predicated on reasonable delay: there was no urgency for Paul to leave Ephesus immediately, and the "great door for effective work" (1 Cor 16:9) was still open to him there. But when Timothy arrived in Corinth, he found the situation beyond his control; and even 1 Corinthians, the apostle's direct missive, failed to make the impact Paul had expected. Whether Timothy returned with this grim report, or Paul found out some other way, the apostle abandoned all plans for delay, and paid an urgent visit instead. This direct confrontation turned out to be a bitter experience, a "painful visit" to use Paul's language (2 Cor 2:1). It may be that some of the abuses treated by Paul in 1 Corinthians had been cleared up; but opposition to him was still very strong, and apparently surfaced in one or two leaders whom the Corinthians either tacitly supported or at least refused to rebuke. Moreover, the church had been infiltrated by Judaizers from Judea, men who were adamantly opposed to the gospel Paul preached and who ridiculed his apostleship. Paul was openly and deeply insulted (2 Cor 2:5-8,10; 7:12); worse, the work of the gospel itself was in jeopardy at Corinth.

Why Paul left at this point and returned in due course to

Ephesus is uncertain. Perhaps he hoped time would heal some of the rift; perhaps he had other pressing engagements. Whatever the reason, he made up his mind not to make another painful visit and therefore called off the double stop he had earlier planned to make at Corinth on his way to and from Macedonia. Ironically, this opened him up to the charge of being fickle and lacking resolution in his plans (2 Cor 1:16-2:4).

But although he refused at this time to return to Corinth in person, he sent another letter, this time by the hands of Titus (who may well have been a more forceful person than Timothy). This third letter we may call Corinthians C; it is sometimes referred to as the severe letter or the tearful letter, for Paul speaks of it along these lines. Like Corinthians A, it has not come down to us, and (along with a lot of other correspondence) was never providentially spared to become part of the New Testament canon. But Paul refers to this lost missive when he writes, "I wrote you out of great distress and anguish of heart and with many tears, not to grieve you but to let you know the depth of my love for you" (2 Cor 2:4); or again, "The reason I wrote you was to see if you would stand the test and be obedient in everything" (vv. 2:9). In this severe letter, Paul had (among other things) demanded the punishment of the ringleader who had opposed him so maliciously (vv. 3,4,6,9; 7:8-12). The context of these passages argues strongly against the view that the severe letter or painful letter was 1 Corinthians, and that the man in question was the church member who was sleeping with his stepmother (1 Cor 5:1-10). The passages in 2 Corinthians that refer to Paul's demand in the severe letter for church discipline give no hint of sexual sin: on the contrary, the offense was against Paul, and the crucial question was whether or not the church would rally around its apostolic founder (e.g., 7:12).

Not only did Paul entrust the painful letter to Titus, he further charged his emissary with the responsibility to organize the collection for the Christians in Jerusalem (2 Cor 8:6). Apparently this plan, introduced earlier, had fallen on hard times, owing in part to the animus some Corinthians nurtured against Paul, but even more to the fact that the interlopers from Judea were demanding financial support (11:7,12-20; 12:14) and were thereby siphoning off funds that should have gone to Jerusalem. Yet the very fact that Paul expected Titus to continue the collection in

Corinth proves that, however disastrous the painful visit had been, the apostle did not regard the church as fundamentally renegade and apostate, but as vacillating, uncertain in its allegiances, too self-assured by half, and much too prone to division and to the toleration, not only of open sinners, but of self-proclaimed leaders who opposed both Paul and his gospel. That is why Paul can still boast of this church's generosity to Titus (7:14) and even to the Macedonians (9:2), even though in certain other respects the church was in a spiritually dangerous situation. (It must be remembered, though, that it was Paul's practice to be grateful and to issue generous encouragement wherever possible among his churches, even when the overall picture was not too bright: witness 1 Cor 1:4-7!) But however qualified, the situation called forth from Paul the severe and painful letter just described.

Meanwhile, Paul continued his ministry in Asia Minor, doubtless focusing his attention on Ephesus. As if the emotional drain caused by the Corinthian church were not enough, during this period he faced some of the worst opposition and most frightening dangers he had ever confronted. He later wrote, "We do not want you to be uninformed, brothers, about the hardships we suffered in the province of Asia. We were under great pressure, far beyond our ability to endure, so that we despaired even of life. Indeed, in our hearts we felt the sentence of death. But this happened that we might not rely on ourselves but on God, who raises the dead. He has delivered us from such a deadly peril (2 Cor 1:8-10). We do not know any details of these dangers; but we do know that shortly after the Demetrius riot (Acts 19:23-20:1) Paul left Ephesus for Troas (2 Cor 2:12,13; the expression might refer either to the port city or to the Troad region in which it lay. Cf. Acts 20:6) where he hoped simultaneously to meet Titus returning with news of Corinth, and to preach the gospel. The latter hope was realized: he found "the Lord had opened a door" (2 Cor 2:12) for him. His other hope remained unfulfilled; and Paul was forced to write, "I still had no peace of mind, because I did not find my brother Titus there" (13).

Apparently Paul and Titus had made contingency plans to meet in Macedonia (perhaps at Philippi) should the meeting in Troas not take place; for that is where Paul headed next, probably as soon as weather permitted navigation, still in hope of meeting

Titus and learning something of the Corinthian response to his severe and painful letter. In Macedonia, Paul took up his pastoral ministry of instruction and encouragement (Acts 20:1,2) while organizing the collection for the Jerusalem believers (2 Cor 8:1-4; 9:2). The work was dangerous and arduous, not least because the Macedonian churches were themselves facing "the most severe trial" and "extreme poverty" (8:2). But worse still, Titus was not to be found. Paul later wrote, "[When] we came into Macedonia, this body of ours had no rest, but we were harassed at every turn—conflicts on the outside, fears within" (7:5).

Mercifully, Titus soon arrived; and his news was so good that Paul's mood changed to near euphoria. "But God," he wrote, "who comforts the downcast, comforted us by the coming of Titus, and not only by his coming but also by the comfort you had given him. He told us about your longing for me, your deep sorrow, your ardent concern for me, so that my joy was greater than ever" (2 Cor 7:6,7). Indeed, after sending off the severe letter, he had immediately regretted it, fearing it would hurt the Corinthians unduly; but now upon learning how effective his letter was, regret is replaced by joy. After all, if his letter hurt them, it was "only for a little while" (v. 8); and in any case, he observes, "Godly sorrow brings repentance that leads to salvation and leaves no regret, but worldly sorrow brings death" (v. 10). Paul's entire response to Titus's report (vv. 5-16) presupposes that the desperate problems in Corinth have been substantially cleared up.

It is at this point that we become less certain of the precise sequence of events. Because this question affects the interpretation of 2 Corinthians 10-13, a brief account must be given of the three principal explanations offered by commentators.

First: Many argue that Paul, overjoyed by Titus's report, immediately wrote 2 Corinthians 1-9 (which thus in effect becomes "Corinthians D"), but that 2 Corinthians 10-13 originally formed no part of this document. Rather, this section is to be identified as Corinthians C, the severe and painful letter.

There is an immediate advantage to this theory. Even a cursory reading of 2 Corinthians shows how different chapters 1-9 are from chapters 10-13. The former are positive, enthusiastic, encouraging, transparently reflecting the good news Titus has brought. If here and there Paul must still provide some account of his movements (1:15-2:13), explain again the nature of apostolic ministry (3:1-18), warn against idolatry (6:14-7:1), and continue his exhortation to organize the collection (chaps. 8-9), all this is written in a tone of joy, of confidence in the church's growing maturity and obedience. The tone is sometimes cautious, but never harsh; and it is frequently euphoric. By contrast, chapters 10-13 presuppose that the situation in Corinth is desperate. The language is intensely emotional, oscillating from angry to broken to ironic. Joy cannot be found, and confidence in the Corinthian church is all but dissipated. No longer does Paul write, "I am glad I can have complete confidence in you" (7:16); now he must say, "Examine yourselves to see whether you are in the faith; test yourselves. Do you not realize that Christ Jesus is in you—unless, of course, you fail the test?" (13:5-6).

Much more can be said in favor of this theory; but it stumbles badly over at least three obstacles. (1) No Greek manuscript of 2 Corinthians suggests the letter originally terminated at the end of chapter 9, or suggests that chapters 10-13 once had an opening salutation typical of the letters Paul writes to churches where he was known. This is not conclusive in itself, of course; one could argue that the appropriate ending and introduction were lost when someone put the two letters together. But in that case, the puzzle is *why* an early reader would want to do such a thing, and why there is *no* trace of it in a very full manuscript tradition. (2) Moreover, 12:18 clearly presupposes that Titus had paid at least one visit to Corinth to assist in the collection—i.e., it presupposes either 8:6a or 8:16-19. Either way, it becomes very difficult to believe that chapters 10-13, the section in which 12:18 is embedded, were penned *before* chapters 1-9. (3) More important, chapters 10-13 do not sound like what we actually know of Corinthians C. One certain feature in that letter is Paul's demand that a certain offender be punished (cf. 2:5,6; 7:12); but there is no trace of this in 2 Corinthians 10-13. Moreover, these chapters promise an imminent visit (12:14; 13:1); yet "Corinthians C, the severe letter, was sent *instead* of a second painful visit (1:23; 2:1). How could Paul boast to Titus (7:14) and the Macedonians (9:2) about the Corinthians' generosity if relations between Paul and the Corinthian church had deteriorated to the point that he was charged with using the collection funds himself (12:16)? And does the tone of 2 Corinthians 10-13—the sustained irony and biting invective—sound as if this passage was composed in the mood portrayed in 2:4—"out of great distress and anguish of heart and with many tears"? Finally, if 2 Corinthians 10-13 were composed before 2 Corinthians 1-9, why do the latter chapters make no mention of the group of interlopers who are so central to the former? Even if the problem had cleared up by the time chapters 1-9 were written, why is that fact not recorded, when the resolution of other and presumably less significant problems is duly recorded? We must reject the view that 2 Corinthians 10-13 is to be identified with Corinthians C.

Second: Many others argue for the essential unity of 2 Corinthians. This obviously squares with the textual evidence; but it must seek some solid reason for the demonstrable change in tone between chapters 1-9 and 10-13. Proposed solutions have varied enormously. Perhaps Paul had a sleepless night, suggests Lietzmann; perhaps Paul finally reveals his deepest and hitherto repressed emotions on these matters (Menzies, Robertson); perhaps this change reflects nothing more than the ups and downs of Paul's temperament (Goudge); or perhaps the differences between chapters 1-9 and chapters 10-13 are greatly exaggerated, and there is really no problem to solve (Hughes— who draws comparisons between 1:13 and 10:11; 1:17 and 10:2; 2:1 and 12:14,21 and 13:1,2; 2:17 and 12:19; 3:2 and 12:11; 6:13 and 11:2 and 12:14; 8:6,8,22 and 12:17,18).

Similar lists of comparisons, however, could be drawn between 2 Corinthians 10-13 and 1 Corinthians (and some of these connections will be drawn out in this exposition); but no one argues that such parallels prove 2 Corinthians 10-13 is really a part of 1 Corinthians. The change of tone between chapters 1-9 and chapters 10-13 is too noticeable to pass over; and the explanations commonly given are not very satisfying. Was Paul so emotionally immature that he could not contain himself? Was his temperament as mercurial as some suggest? After all, the change in tone extends to his *pastoral stance* toward the Corinthians: chapters 1-9 find Paul essentially building up the Corinthians, building bridges toward them, and even the rebukes are part of that design; whereas chapters 10-13 find Paul tearing down the Corinthians with irony, rebuking them sharply, and even the brief words of encouragement constitute part of that

pattern. At very least, it seems necessary to suppose that there
was a change in the pastoral problem Paul was confronting.

Such a possibility brings us to some form of the next
explanation:

Third: Many commentators have suggested that 2 Corinthians
10-13 was written somewhat later than chapters 1-9. According
to this view Titus met Paul in Macedonia (as described, above),
and Paul was so encouraged he immediately wrote off to the
Corinthian church. What he wrote, however, was not all of 2
Corinthians, but only 2 Corinthians 1-9 (Corinthians D). Later on,
he learned that the report brought by Titus was either
premature or obsolete: the fickle Corinthians were succumbing
to pressures introduced by interlopers from Judea and reverting
to their carping criticism of the apostle, their earlier lack of
discipline, and their pagan arrogance. Paul therefore responds
with a stinging letter, our 2 Corinthians 10-13 (which thus
becomes Corinthians E—so Barrett, Bruce).

There is much to commend this explanation. It avoids
identifying 2 Corinthians 10-13 with Corinthians C, the severe
letter; and it adequately explains why chapters 10-13 are so
different in tone from 1-9. But in its most common form, it
suffers from one or two of the weaknesses of the first solution,
already discussed: it must suppose, without any manuscript
evidence, that both the ending of chapters 1-9 and the beginning
of chapters 10-13 were somehow lost, and that the two sections
were put together. At least in this theory they are put together
in the right sequence! Those who argue for the thorough unity
of this epistle (the second explanation, discussed above) might
also ask how come the Corinthians fell away so quickly, and why
there is no explicit reference in chapters 10-13 to the more
recent news Paul allegedly received informing him the situation
was much bleaker than he thought. Indeed, Harris suggests that
Paul did not write any part of 2 Corinthians right after hearing
Titus's good report. Rather, Harris argues, Paul continued his
pastoral work in Macedonia, and quite possibly pursued a
ministry of pioneer evangelism along the Egnatian Way and
right around to Illyricum (cf. Rom 15:19-21); and he did not write
2 Corinthians until he returned to Macedonia once more and
heard of fresh problems in Corinth.

Harris's reconstruction is certainly possible; but it must

minimize the change of tone between the two sections. It loses
the strength of the suggestion that what prompts the change is
the arrival of more information, the receipt of bad news, since
on Harris's view the bad news arrives before Paul writes any
part of 2 Corinthians. On this interpretation one might have
expected Paul to have maintained something of the same stance
toward his readers throughout his epistle.

But perhaps we may put together the strengths of the second
and the third explanations. If Paul was as eager to hear from
Titus as he seems to have been it is hard to believe that he could
set off on further pastoral and evangelistic rounds without
preparing any response to the Corinthians at all. Grateful that
his severe letter had not done the damage he feared, delighted
that repentance and obedience had been reestablished in the
Corinthian church, and encouraged to think that healthy
relationships were being restored, he immediately began to write
(or dictate). But 2 Corinthians is a fairly long letter: few could
manage to write it at a lengthy single sitting. And Paul was at
the time (it will be remembered) extraordinarily pressed by his
ministry in Macedonia; lengthy sessions in which to compose one's
thoughts would not be easy to come by. Perhaps the completion
of the letter was repeatedly delayed, for weeks or even longer.
Most of us, after all, have occasionally put off finishing a letter,
doubtless a letter a good deal shorter than 2 Corinthians. In this
case, however, Paul may well have received additional news, bad
news about the Corinthian church, before he had finished the
letter; and if so, this would account for the abrupt change of
tone at the beginning of chapter 10. In short, after finishing the
first nine chapters, but before actually terminating the letter and
sending it off, Paul receives additional bad news, and therefore
adds four more chapters of rebuke. Second Corinthians is thus
a formally unified letter, but does reflect a substantial change
of perspective in the last four chapters.

Four principal objections frequently raised against this
reconstruction merit brief consideration.

(1) Barrett, adhering to the third interpretation, argues that
if chapters 1-9 had not already been sent off when the bad news
arrived, prompting Paul to write chapters 10-13, the apostle
would have torn up those earlier chapters as already out of date,
and would simply have replaced them with the sharper accents

of 2 Corinthians 10-13. There is some force to this argument; but it overlooks how much in 2 Corinthians is valuable in its own right, and still applicable to the Corinthians even when their situation is deteriorating. This useful material includes, among other things, the glory of the ministry (chap. 3), warnings against idolatry (6:14-7:1), and instructions regarding the collection (chaps. 8-9). Even the haunting words about Paul's joy when he hears the Corinthians are repentant, obedient, and zealous might serve as an added rebuke when they are that way *no longer.*

(2) Some argue that the movements of Titus and an unnamed brother, spoken of in 2 Corinthians 12:18 as having already taken place, are to be identified with Titus's *future* movements in 8:17,18. If so, then 2 Corinthians 1-9 *must* have been sent *before* 2 Corinthians 10-13 was written. I shall say more about this when we get to 12:18; but for now it is worth mentioning that this verse *may* look back, not on 8:16,17 but on 8:6a—a trip Titus had already taken, probably in connection with the severe letter, and certainly before *any part* of 2 Corinthians was penned. If so, there is no need to postulate a break after chapter 9.

(3) Others express surprise that the Corinthian church could relapse so quickly, and fall into a condition no better and perhaps considerably worse than that which called forth the earlier severe and painful letter. But surely the speed with which the Corinthians fell is not all that remarkable. After all, 1 Corinthians does not encourage us to think Paul was dealing with a mature and stable church, but with one filled with assorted forms of arrogance and a remarkable penchant for blind and exclusivistic attachment to one leader or another (e.g., 1 Cor 1:10-17). Certainly 2 Corinthians 10-13 testifies to the new credibility and power of the interlopers, self-proclaimed leaders who captured a substantial portion of Corinthian opinion and turned many of the believers against Paul and his gospel. Quite possibly fresh strength had come to these self-promoted leaders by the arrival of new forces from Jerusalem. In any case, their multiplying influence was the new situation introduced into this immature church; and the dismal record of the Corinthians in practical discernment practically guaranteed they would be dupes, dangerous dupes, once again.

(4) The only really serious difficulty with this interpretation is that 2 Corinthians 10-13 nowhere explicitly states that Paul

actually did receive new information, information that caused him to change his tone from gentleness to the sting of a whip (cf. 1 Cor 4:21). Even so, this single difficulty is in my judgment less awkward than those attached to the alternative explanations. Intelligent speculation as to *why* Paul fails to mention the arrival of such new information is not hard to come by. For instance, if the new information about the Corinthian church came in a report (known to many members of the church) that accused Paul, among other things, of acting with too much "meekness and gentleness" instead of with the forcefulness demanded of a true apostle, then Paul's opening words in 2 Corinthians 10:1 would be sufficient to draw attention to that report: "By the meekness and gentleness of Christ, I appeal to you. . . ." This same argument could be strengthened many times if the report of bad news included, e.g., insinuations that Paul did not fare well when compared with the interlopers (cf. 10:12-18), that he could not be much of a teacher since he refused to charge for his services (cf. 11:7-12; 12:13), or that his apostolic status was inferior because he seldom seemed to talk of the glorious supernatural visions of which others could fondly speak (cf. 12:1-10). If Paul were responding to some such attack as this, which seems likely, his very response was sufficient indication that the new report had reached him. To draw any further attention to it would have been a redundant exercise.

On the whole, therefore, it seems best to conclude that 2 Corinthians 10-13 is formally part of 2 Corinthians (= Corinthians D), even though its emphases and tone set it somewhat apart from the rest of the book. At several steps in the argument, the evidence suffers from enough ambiguity to restrain us from being too dogmatic on the fine points; but it is sufficient to enable us to treat 2 Corinthians 10-13 as a conceptual unit worthy of close study. That is all I need to establish here: these four chapters stand slightly apart, and constitute an impressive display of the apostle Paul's reponse under withering fire.

Thus we come to the second question:

B. What Is the Precise Nature of the Opposition Paul Faces?

Most of the details of the opposition Paul confronts will be fleshed in by the exposition; but it may be useful to reconnoiter a little and outline both the essence of the attack and the identity of the opponents.

1. The essence of the attack. Paul faces intruders whose fundamental aim is to call his authority into question, while magnifying their own (2 Cor 10:7-18). If they succeed in their efforts, they will woo the Corinthians' allegiance to themselves. Paul, they said, is personally unimpressive, and his oratory substandard (v. 10). He could command respect only at a distance (vv. 1-2, 9-11; 11:6; 13:3-4,9): his letters might be forceful, but they outstrip the credibility of his person and are therefore of little consequence. Paul could thus be charged with acting inconsistently, even capriciously (vv. 2-4; cf. 1:17-18). His problem, they say, is that he lacks proper credentials: he does not even bother to present the appropriate letters of introduction and commendation, presumably from the Twelve (10:13-14; cf. 3:1). He has to rely on self-commendation (10:12-18; 12:11; cf. 5:12; 6:4-10).

Thus Paul finds himself between the proverbial rock and a hard place: he is not forceful enough when present, yet if he writes a forceful response his letter will be easily dismissed as further evidence of the fact that only by long distance mail can he sound like a leader; and even then his words might be dismissed as self-commendation. If instead he shows up in person, he himself is forced to admit that he does not meet the prevalent standards of rhetoric (2 Cor 11:6), so he may appear hopelessly outclassed by the intruders. Worse, he may be handicapped by his memory of the "painful visit" (2:1), and therefore pull his punches—which would only serve to confirm the judgment of his attackers: "His letters are weighty and forceful, but in person he is unimpressive and his speaking amounts to nothing" (10:10). But if he does nothing, he will certainly lose the Corinthians to the influence of the intruders.

There are other and equally vicious pairs of charges leveled against Paul, pairs of charges that make rebuttal extremely difficult—like a lone infantryman answering machine-gun crossfire. On the one hand, Paul is charged with the "sin" of refusing to receive financial help from the Corinthians, who felt slighted because of this policy and questioned Paul's credentials as a result (e.g., 11:5,7-11; 12:11-15; 13:3a,6). Surely, the Corinthians reasoned, a great apostle, a truly significant teacher, would charge in proportion to his worth; so if Paul not only refuses to levy a charge but turns down every offer of a gift, it must be because he is counterfeit. Yet at the same time, at least some Corinthians had become convinced that the collection Paul was urging them to set aside on a regular basis for the impoverished Jerusalem Christians (1 Cor 16:1-4; 2 Cor 8-9) was in reality a fraudulent way of lining his own pockets (12:16-18)! So once again Paul is squeezed between two antithetical demands: if he continues to refuse all financial help, he will be dismissed as an inferior apostle, a second-class teacher; while if he reverses policy, his action will be condemned as confirmation of his suspected avarice.

At the root of these multifaceted attacks lies the problem of *boasting* (a word repeated many times in these four chaps). Paul's opponents were apparently swayed by sophists who were prominent throughout Greece, and perhaps nowhere more so than in Corinth. The self-proclaimed "apostles" who attacked Paul, not only adopted the Hellenistic standards of rhetoric best exemplified in the sophists, but went further: they also took over the sophists' penchant for self-commendation and their insistence on payment. Sophists delighted to parade their accomplishments and display their oratory. They aimed to collect a growing number of disciples who hung on their words and paid large sums for the privilege of learning at their feet. The more accomplished the sophist, the more he could boast, and the greater the charge he could levy. Sophisticated haughtiness became a virtue, self-admiration a strength. The sophist Polemon "used to talk to cities as a superior, to kings as not inferior, and to gods as an equal" (*Vit. Soph.* 1.25.4). Philostratus testifies that "a sophist is put out in an extempore speech by a serious-looking audience and tardy praise and no clapping" (2.26.3). This attitude prevailed in circles beyond the sophists: the Roman historian Tacitus explains, "In the scorn of fame was implied the scorn of virtue" (*Ann.* 4.38). Great leaders not infrequently wrote memoirs of their exploits that were nothing more than self-eulogies, detailing the triumphs gained, the battles won, the great speeches delivered, the wisdom displayed, the captives subdued.[1]

This same professional stance, adopted unquestioningly by the interlopers and adapted to their own religious environment, was part of what motivated them to belittle Paul for his less than acceptable rhetoric, his refusal to receive payment for his services, his serious lack of personal impressiveness. When had Paul ever provided a suitable list of his accomplishments (cf. 2 Cor 11:16-29)? And if he were such a great apostle, why had he not received spectacular visions from God and enhanced his credibility by relating them (12:1-10)?

Quite clearly the Corinthians were culturally conditioned to be led astray in these directions. Even in his first canonical letter to them, Paul found it necessary to explain very carefully that he had not preached the gospel with the "eloquence" of the approved rhetoric, that he had not adopted the "superior wisdom" characterized by self-promotion (1 Cor 2:1). Far from it: he had already resolved to avoid such approaches and focus instead on Jesus Christ and his crucifixion—a stumbling block to Jews and foolishness to Gentiles (1:23). Arrogance was at this point of his ministry a stranger to Paul: he arrived in Corinth "in weakness and fear, and with much trembling" (2:3), so much so that, as we have seen, God graciously gave him special encouragement (Acts 18:9,10). None of this was accidental: it was shaped by God toward one crucial end. "My message and my preaching," Paul explains, "were not with wise and persuasive words, but with a demonstration of the Spirit's power, *so that your faith might not rest on men's wisdom, but on God's power*" (1 Cor 2:4).

Sadly, the Corinthian Christians did not learn this lesson very quickly. Their minds were shaped rather more by their pagan culture than by the gospel of Jesus Christ; and therefore many of them were swayed by the interlopers, seduced into another

---

1. On this background, see J. Munck, *Paul and the Salvation of Mankind* (London: SCM, 1959) 158; S. H. Travis, "Paul's Boasting in 2 Corinthians 10-12," *Studia Evangelica VI* (Berlin: Akademie-Verlag, 1973) 527-32, and the literature there cited; and esp. three articles by E. A. Judge, "The Early Christians as a Scholastic Community: Part II," *Journal of Religious History* 1 (1960-61) 125-37; "The Conflict of Aims in NT Thought," *Journal of Christian Education* 9 (1966) 32-45; "Paul's Boasting in Relation to Contemporary Professional Practice," *Australian Biblical Review* 16 (1968) 37-50.

form of the same error that Paul by his example and his epistolary instruction had already condemned. Perhaps what made the Corinthians blind to the danger was the fact that these intruders did not align themselves with the pagan sophists, but with Christians: indeed, they had the highest Christian credentials. It is always much more difficult for Christians to detect a fundamentally sinful attitude in other Christians than in pagans—especially if that attitude is endemic to contemporary society, thereby reducing or eliminating the "shock" force of that sin. Certainly the men who led the Corinthians astray were less interested in weighing Paul's claims and responses in an even-handed way than were the Corinthians themselves: as far as we can discern it, their attitude toward Paul was shaped by the raw triumphalism of the sophists. Far from being even-handed, they were consistently demeaning and condescending.

If the entire situation had been nothing more than a personality conflict in which Paul came out worst, it is very doubtful that he would have responded as forcefully as he does in these four chapters. Paul was painfully aware that the lot of the apostle was to "become the scum of the earth, the refuse of the world" (1 Cor 4:13). More excruciating, but still expected, was the constant "danger from false brothers" (2 Cor 11:26). But this situation was going beyond even that. Not only were the attitudes and values being inculcated by the intruders so deeply pagan, so intrinsically self-centered, that the Corinthians were being warped and twisted away from deep, experiential knowledge of the love and strength of the God whose "power is made perfect in weakness" (12:9), but these self-promoted leaders were actually peaching another Jesus than the one Paul had preached—a different spirit and a different gospel (11:4). Paul was not reacting merely out of hurt feelings (though doubtless his feelings were hurt), but out of the passionate perception that the gospel itself was at stake—and with it the eternal well-being of the Corinthians. That is why he can go so far as to say, "Examine yourselves to see whether you are in the faith; test yourselves." Where the essence of the gospel is the issue, Paul habitually draws very sharp lines of distinction (e.g., Gal 1:8-9); so it is not surprising that in this case he exposes the intruders as "false apostles, deceitful workmen, masquerading as apostles of Christ" (11:13).

2. The identity of the opponents. Enough has already been said about them that they have begun to take shape; but three further observations will bring their picture into sharper focus.

First, the terms "intruders" and "interlopers" were not inadvertent slips. Paul's chief opponents in 2 Corinthians 10-13 were not native to the Corinthian church, but people who entered it as latecomers and quickly gained positions of leadership and voices of authority. This is made clear not only by strong hints in several passages (e.g., 10:13-15; 11:4; 12:11), but also by the theme of commendation; the intruders apparently delighted in parading letters of introduction and commendation. They insinuated that Paul's credentials were questionable because he did not follow the same practice. To present themselves in this way, the opponents must have been outsiders.

This means that they are not to be identified with any of the problematic factions reflected in 1 Corinthians, where the warring groups were all within the church and native to it (even if each faction adopted the name of some leader whose origins were elsewhere). There may, of course, be a link between the intruders in 2 Corinthians 10-13 and one or more of the parties described in 1 Corinthians 1:11 (Allo suggests the "Christ party," Barrett the "Peter party"); but such connections are speculative.

Second, although, as we have seen, the intruders were mightily influenced by what we might call a sophist mentality, nevertheless it is no less certain that they were Jews: nothing could be clearer from 2 Corinthians 10:22. Some scholars have therefore suggested that they were Hellenistic-Jewish preachers who professed to be Christians but were in reality trying to take over the Christian community with their own doctrine, claiming to be "divine men." But there are problems with the "divine man" category;[2] and even if the category were well established, the normal profile of such self-proclaimed leaders would not encourage us to suspect they would flourish letters of commendation. Far from it: they would claim independence from men

2. It is often argued that the *theios anē* ("divine man") was a common and understood category of self-proclaimed religious hero and itinerant preacher in the Hellenistic world; but the evidence is scanty, and the designation inconsistent in its referent: cf. esp. Carl H. Holladay, *Theios Aner in Hellenistic Judaism: A Critique of the Use of This Category in New Testament Christology* (Missoula: Scholars, 1977).

and parade their miraculous stunts as the sole credentials that might be needed.

The best guess is that the interlopers were some brand of Judaizers. This is not difficult to accept, if we remember four things:

(1) As the early church reached more and more Gentiles with the good news of Jesus Christ, many devout Jews who were prepared to accept Jesus as Messiah but who were not prepared to see him as the fulfillment of the Mosaic law began to insist with increasing stridency that any Gentile who wanted to follow Jesus Messiah had to obey the law of Moses. Those who held this position came in time to be called Judaizers. The precise nature of their demands varied: in Galatia, e.g., they insisted that Gentiles be circumcised and thus bind themselves to obey the entire law of Moses (cf. Gal 5:2-6; 6:12-15), even the special Jewish festivals (Gal 4:10). The Book of Acts makes it clear that at certain stages in Paul's missionary career Jews dogged Paul's steps and attempted to undermine his message of grace.

(2) We must beware of thinking that there was only one kind of Jewish party that stood over against Christianity. There were as many different opinions among Jews then as there are now, and they could merge and blend in surprising combinations. No one familiar with the first century would be surprised to find a Hellenistic-Jewish chief priest by the name of Sceva deeply involved in exorcism practices of dubious credentials (Acts 19:13-16). In Colosse, opposition to Paul's doctrines surfaced among Jews who, though they had been influenced by pagan notions, nevertheless insisted on observing the Jewish feasts. In short, what was characteristic of Judaizing was not a coherent system of thought, but a common attempt to impose Jewish practices and all or part of the Mosaic law upon Gentiles as conditions for salvation or at least for Christian maturity. Thus it is not difficult to imagine Hellenistic Jews who, precisely because they were thoroughly Hellenistic, took over many of the attitudes of their surrounding society (best exemplified in this instance by the sophists); yet precisely because they were thoroughly Jews, they felt tied to the same stance toward Jesus (and what it means for a Gentile to become a Christian) that other Judaizers adopted.

Alternatively, one could easily imagine a group of Palestinian

Jews (see 4 below) who had made Christian professions of faith and who had lived under Greek influence for enough years to be strongly influenced by the sophists, yet who retained their allegiance to Judaizing principles.

(3) Certainly wherever Paul detected Judaizing he treated it as a heresy. Judaizing, of course, is not the same as Judaism; those who followed the traditional religion of the Jews (i.e., Judaism) Paul regarded as unconverted, in need of repentance and faith in Jesus. Toward such people Paul could be extraordinarily flexible (1 Cor 9:19-23), going so far as to join in Jewish purification rites (Acts 21:20-26), and circumcising Timothy to avoid offending Jewish sensibilities. Nor is Judaizing an apt term to describe the worship and attitude of countless thousands of Jews who truly trusted Jesus the Messiah but who did not give up the traditional observances of Judaism: most Jerusalem Christians fell into this category, and even in Antioch Paul does not object to the presence of a "circumcision group" that eats separately from other Christians. Judaizing refers to the pressure exerted by putative Jewish Christians on Gentile Christians to compel the latter to conform to the whole or to some part of the Mosaic law, as a necessary condition for salvation or Christian maturity. Judaizers therefore operated *within* the Christian camp and were commonly accepted as Christians; but Paul perceived that as soon as they insisted that something *in addition to* Christ was necessary for salvation or Christian growth, they were destroying the fundamental structure of Christianity as he understood it. Grace would no longer be grace; merit theology would insert its nose into the tent, like the proverbial camel. That is why Paul pronounces his repeated "anathema" on the Judaizers in Galatia (Gal 1:8-9).

(4) The two crucial verses in 2 Corinthians 10-13 that bear on this question are 11:4 and 11:22. In the former, Paul insists that the intruders were preaching another Jesus than the one Paul preached, a different spirit and a different gospel from those the Corinthians had received. The language is reminiscent of Galatians 1:8,9, and is typical of Paul's known attitude toward Judaizers. In 2 Corinthians 11:22, Paul rhetorically asks, "Are they Hebrews?" And he answers, "So am I." But the word "Hebrews" is normally restricted to those Jews whose linguistic heritage was Hebrew/Aramaic—i.e., those from Palestine. On

this basis some commentators argue that the intruders were born and reared in Palestine, and were probably such latecomers to Corinth that it is not easy to believe they could have fallen under strong influence from the sophists. But this interpretation overlooks Paul's "So am I"; for Paul was *not* born in Palestine, but in the Hellenistic city of Tarsus. Paul may have been reared in Palestine, but certainly he gained enough Greek education to be able to cite minor poets such as Epimenides (Acts 17:28; cf. Titus 1:12). His point in 2 Corinthians 11:22, however, is that he was brought up to speak Hebrew/Aramaic and so to share in the full theological heritage that such linguistic competence would make possible. By the same token, the intruders may or may not have been born in Palestine. Like Paul, they might have been "Hebrews" in that they too were thoroughly conversant with the language and culture of Palestine, even though they were born and reared in more Hellenistic surroundings. What seems reasonably clear is that they were Judaizers with Palestinian training and at least some sophist attitudes. How that precise combination came about we can only guess.

These intruders may be like those people from Judea who had earlier invoked the authority of the Twelve without in fact gaining their approval (Acts 15:24). After all, one faction at Corinth had already used the name of Peter (cf. 1 Cor 1:12). To the Corinthians, such authority would bear great weight. If Paul's gospel was to be overthrown, Paul's authority would have to be called into question. How better to achieve this end, from the Jewish side, then by appealing to all the Jerusalem associations that would resonate with authority in the ears of all early Christians, and from the Greek side by advancing a phalanx of objections against Paul that would instantly appear plausible because of the built-in cultural bias?

The *third* observation is that the number of groups Paul refers to is disputed. Several recent commentators have argued for three groups. First and foremost, of course, are the Corinthians themselves. Paul is sometimes angry with them, and constantly grieves over them; but because he recognizes that they are the dupes of the intruders, he never handles them quite as harshly as he does his prime opponents. Those opponents are the second group—the "false apostles" (2 Cor 11:13) who have introduced "a different gospel" (11:4). They have seduced the Corinthians and managed to nurture seeds of suspicion in their minds as to the status and integrity of Paul. But third, there are what Barrett calls "apostles of recognized eminence"—i.e., the Twelve themselves. Barrett, followed by Bruce and Harris, argue that the "super-apostles" in 11:5 and 12:11 are not the *false* apostles but the Twelve whom the intruders invoke in order to gain respectability and authority. When Paul discusses the false apostles he dismisses them as Satan's minions, and ominously concludes, "Their end will be what their actions deserve" (11:13-15). But when Paul mentions the "super-apostles" (11:5; 12:11), he goes no further than to say he is not in the least inferior to them.

This interpretation is quite plausible; and if correct, it helps to explain Paul's embarrassed position. For if the intruders were pushing not only themselves, but also the Jerusalem apostles, seeking to raise their own stature by claiming (however falsely) to represent the Twelve, Paul is in a cleft stick: he must expose the sham of the intruders without diminishing the authority of the Twelve who (apparently) recommended them.

Yet I remain unpersuaded that we should interpret 2 Corinthians 11:5 and 12:11 in this way. Rather, the "super-apostle" designation is better taken as a further ironic reference to the false apostles. There are four reasons to support this judgment:

(1) The central section of 2 Corinthians 10-12 is made up of Paul's boasting (11:16-12:10), a passage steeped in irony. When in this passage he asks questions such as "Are they Hebrews?" or "Are they servants of Christ?" (11:22,23), the "they" in view are the false apostles of the immediately preceding verses (11:13-15). But immediately after this long section on boasting, written to stifle the false apostles, Paul concludes, "I have made a fool of myself, but you drove me to it. I ought to have been commended by you, for I am not in the least inferior to the 'super-apostles', even though I am nothing" (12:11). Because the boasting section *begins* with a reference to the false apostles, the most natural way of understanding 12:11ff. is that it *concludes* the boasting section with a reference to the same people under the ironic designation "super-apostle." If so, the same designation in 11:4 should probably be interpreted the same way.

(2) There is more irony in 2 Corinthians 10-13 than in all the

rest of Paul's extant writings combined. Therefore there is ample contextual reason for thinking that "super-apostle" should be handled ironically as well.

(3) When elsewhere Paul is forced to draw some sort of comparison between himself and the Twelve (or the Jerusalem "pillars" more generally), he normally makes explicit reference to the people to whom he is referring (e.g., Gal 2:6-10; 1 Cor 15:5,9). There is nothing so explicit here. Indeed, because Paul has had to compare himself with the intruders, the false apostles (e.g., 2 Cor 10:12-18; 11:16-12:10), in order to secure the allegiance of the Corinthians to the gospel, we must imagine his rebuke to the Corinthians, "I ought to have been commended by you" (12:11), means something like "I ought to have been commended by you before the interlopers, so their personal pretensions would have been for naught." But that crucial clause in 12:11 must be interpreted by Barrett, Bruce, and Harris to mean something like "I ought to have been commended by you before the interlopers, so that their claims that I am inferior to the Twelve would be exposed as untrue." The latter interpretation would make sense only if Paul had already presented lengthy comparisons between himself and the Twelve; but that is precisely what he has not done.

(4) There is no reason to think that the claims of these Judaizers to represent some authority in Jerusalem were valid. Along similar lines, it is very doubtful if Peter or Apollos were personally behind the factions mentioned in 1 Corinthians 1:12; rather, misguided people invoked their names and authority and did considerable damage. Certainly Paul's earliest run-ins with Judaizers who claimed the authority of the Jerusalem leaders would have taught him that the Jerusalem leaders preferred to disavow such connections. They themselves declared, "We have heard that some went out from us without our authorization and disturbed you" (Acts 15:24). Therefore it is unlikely Paul would have believed the credentials of the intruders in Corinth; and for that reason he would not have felt too pressured to stroke the feathers of the great names connected with Jerusalem. In other words, Paul would have been in a more difficult position if he believed the credentials were valid but the messengers had gone bad; but based on his earlier experiences it is unlikely Paul would have believed the credentials to be

authentic. In that case, there would be very little reason to drag the Jerusalem leaders into the discussion at all.

This sketch of the background of 2 Corinthians 10-13 has gone on long enough: I must draw it to a close and get on with the exposition. Yet this introduction should lead us to anticipate from these chapters of Scripture some light on several crucial topics:

(1) We shall learn something of apostleship, and, derivatively, of the nature of Christian leadership. Little is more important in our age, in which promoting self under the guise of promoting Christ has become, not only commonplace, but a defended practice in books and seminars on Christian leadership. Paul's authoritative grasp of the topic is profoundly humbling.

(2) We shall discover the evil intrinsic to much boasting, and the way it is deeply related to the self-centeredness that lies at the heart of *all* sin. Modern "Christian" success formulas, too frequently developed by hucksters of glamor marketed by Madison Avenue techniques, pandering to personal comfort and aggrandizement, and formulated to mesh smoothly with our pagan society's idea of the heroic, reveal more about triumphalism than the way of the cross. One recent book sports the nearly blasphemous title, *How to Write Your Own Ticket with God.* Another presents what it calls the "law of reciprocity" to encourage the believer that the more you give the more you get. There is just enough truth in the idea to make the presentation believable to the gullible; but Luke 6:36-38 is made to sound as if the fundamental *reason* for giving is getting (which neither this passage nor any other teaches), or that the "law" of reciprocity is so universal a precept, so independent from other teaching in Scripture, that it admits no qualification or balance. We are told that kindness shown to our enemies *inevitably* (after all, this is a law!) results in kindness returned. Why, then, did Jesus go to the cross? Was it perhaps that he himself failed to show enough kindness? Why does he say that his followers must *expect* to be abused, persecuted, hated by all men (e.g., Matt 5:10-12; 10:16-39; 24:9-14; John 15:18-16:4; cf. 2 Tim 3:12-13)? The authors go on to encourage us to believe that the more money we give away, the more we'll have. But perhaps the "repayment" of which Jesus speaks is not always in exact kind; perhaps an eschatological orientation in Jesus' teaching encourages us to think that reward

in many cases comes in the new heaven and the new earth—
not least when it is presaged by martyrdom! Will struggling Third
World Christians who give sacrificially and lovingly to the work
of the Lord, even of their substance, be greatly impressed by
distorted triumphalist interpretations that promise boundless
material wealth? Will Christians under totalitarian regimes,
brothers and sisters in Christ who have lost goods, opportunities
for education and employment, and sometimes life itself, swallow
so fundamentally unbiblical and shallow a notion of reciprocity?
Of course, God is no man's debtor; but frequently his "reward"
is the grace that endures opposition and hardship, and grows in
character, depth, godliness, and understanding—not the glib
promise of temporal power, health, and wealth. To such issues,
2 Corinthians 10-13 speaks trenchantly, and offers a way of
looking at triumphalism that is disturbingly Christian, profoundly
moving, and utterly demanding.

(3) Related to this last point is the model of Christian maturity
Paul provides. Here is a man who sees beyond issues of
personality to the nature of the apostolic gospel and of apostolic
authority. Here is a man who hates to boast, but whose
profound concern for and grasp of the gospel forces him to step
outside his own skin, as it were, to handle a pastoral problem
of immense complexity and delicacy. Here is an apostle who is
fully prepared to serve as the scum of the earth, the refuse of
the world, but whose outstanding feature to Christians with any
depth of understanding is his almost incredible spiritual,
emotional, and intellectual maturity.

(4) We shall learn, too, that individual Christians and local
churches alike must take responsibility for the styles of
leadership they follow. If it is true that Christian leaders are
responsible before God for the teaching they provide, the models
they display, and the directions they take, it is no less true that
Christians and Christian assemblies are responsible for choosing
what and whom they will emulate. The problems at Corinth
depicted in 2 Corinthians 10-13 would never have arisen if the
Corinthian church had handled the intruders in a mature and
biblical fashion in the first place. That they failed to do so reflects
their spiritual immaturity, their unsettling inability to perceive
that the norms of their own society were deeply pagan and not
to be nurtured in the church.

(5) We shall be reminded once more that the early church was not an amalgam of ideal congregations, but, as today, a called-out community of pilgrims whose allegiance is to Jesus Christ but whose maturity is often wanting. Infiltrated by imposters and seduced by siren voices to follow cheaply Christianized versions of what they were already used to from their pagan past, the Corinthian believers remind us that perfection awaits the parousia. Meanwhile, Henry's wisdom remains: "Let not any ministers of Christ think strange, if they meet with perils, not only from enemies, but from false brethren; for blessed Paul himself did so."

Disobedience Versus Discipline
An Appeal for Obedient Faith

2 Corinthians 10:1-6

¹ By the meekness and gentleness of Christ, I appeal to you—I, Paul, who am "timid" when face to face with you, but "bold" when away! ² I beg you that when I come I may not have to be as bold as I expect to be toward some people who think that we live by the standards of this world. ³ For though we live in the world, we do not wage war as the world does. ⁴ The weapons we fight with are not the weapons of the world. On the contrary, they have divine power to demolish strongholds. ⁵ We demolish arguments and every pretension that sets itself up against the knowledge of God, and we take captive every thought to make it obedient to Christ. ⁶ And we will be ready to punish every act of disobedience, once your obedience is complete.

These opening six verses introduce us to several of the themes found in the ensuing four chapters: the charge that Paul is inconsistent, bold when absent and timid when present; the fundamental misunderstanding of Paul's ministry still entertained by the Corinthians; the implicit threat bound up with Paul's impending visit. But above all, these verses present a sharp contrast between the actual situation in the Corinthian church, and what Paul insists should dominate the church. It is the contrast between discipline and disobedience; and, Paul implies, if the discipline has not been reestablished by the time he arrives, he will use his spiritual weapons to impose it. For the moment, he makes a preliminary appeal for obedient faith.

A. An Ironical Prelude (v. 1)

In an abrupt fashion, Paul addresses the entire church at Corinth: the plural "you" ("I appeal to you") forbids us from thinking Paul is addressing only one schismatic part, perhaps the lunatic fringe. Both usage (compare "you" in 2 Cor 12:19 and 13:11-13) and the context (see my comments on 10:6) make it clear that Paul is writing to the Corinthian church as a whole. This writing is an appeal: "I appeal to you," he says. But the content of that appeal awaits verse 2. Before unveiling that content, Paul opens up with this ironical prelude (v. 1).

The irony turns on two factors. First, despite the fact that the Corinthians have charged Paul with being bold and strong only in his letters (2 Cor 10:1,10), Paul in writing this letter refuses to rise to the bait and blast his readers with an apostolic command. Rather, he appeals to them: the verb suggests he urges them, beseeches them. The language is emotional, betraying deep conviction coupled with a profound desire to be heard and understood: literally rendered, the text reads "*I, Paul, I myself*, appeal to you." No longer does Paul associate Timothy with him in his appeal (as in 2 Cor 1:1). Rather, he speaks and writes alone, urgently, personally, and intensely appealing to the Corinthians instead of standing aloof and presenting a severe front. In the only other places where Paul piles these words together—"I, Paul, I myself" (Gal 5:2; 1 Thess 2:18)—he is equally intense and personal.

The second ironical feature about this prelude is Paul's careful identification of that by which he makes his appeal: "*By the meekness and gentleness of Christ*, I appeal to you." He might have said, "As an apostle of the risen and sovereign Christ I command you"; or "By the authority of the sovereign Lord who has commissioned me as his apostle, I order you"; but instead he writes, "By the meekness and gentleness of Christ, I appeal to you." In this way Paul simultaneously provides a counter-example to the charge that his letters are invariably bold, weighty, and forceful (2 Cor 10:1,10), and reminds his readers that if he, Paul, is sometimes charged with timidity in his personal dealings, he is merely following the example of the Lord Jesus himself. Could not Jesus during the days of his earthly ministry openly testify, "Take my yoke upon you and learn from me, for I am gentle and humble in heart" (Matt 11:29)? True, Paul could be very stern both in letter and in person. On another occasion, he wrote, "What do you prefer? Shall I come to you with a whip, or in love and with a gentle spirit?" (1 Cor 4:21). But then again, Jesus himself could present a stern face, not only in public denunciation of religious leaders (Matt 23) but also in strategic actions such as the cleansing of the temple (chap. 21:12,13 and parallels). Although different situations may call forth from wise leaders very different responses, Paul understands that what was characteristic of Jesus' public ministry was meekness and gentleness; and he believes the same characteristics must stamp his own ministry. In Jesus' case, this fundamental attitude of self-emptying achieved its most magnificent splendor in the breathtaking descent from the glory the Son shared with his Father (John 17:5) to the ignominy, shame, and rejection of the cross—a theme celebrated by Paul elsewhere (Phil 2:6-8). Small wonder each of Jesus' followers must take up his own cross (Mark 8:34-38) if he expects to be called a disciple at all, and not forfeit his soul.

Few people understand this essential ingredient of Christianity better than Paul. Not only does meekness appear as a recurring virtue in his letters (Gal 5:23; 6:1; Col 3:12), but entire paragraphs from his pen demonstrate how his theological reflections and his lifestyle supported and confirmed each other. Several of the most moving of these paragraphs are directed to the Corinthians, almost as if they were in need of perpetual reminders of this essential element in the faith they professed. In his first canonical epistle to them, Paul wrote, "For it seems to me that God has put us apostles on display at the end of the procession, like men condemned to die in the arena. . . . To this very hour we go hungry and thirsty, we are in rags, we are brutally treated, we are homeless. We work hard with our own hands. When we are cursed, we bless; when we are persecuted, we endure it; when we are slandered, we answer kindly. Up to this moment we have become the scum of the earth, the refuse of the world" (1 Cor 4:9,11-13). The same attitude of service and commitment is now repeated in Paul's second canonical Epistle to the Corinthians: "We put no stumbling block in anyone's path, so that our ministry will not be discredited. Rather, as servants of God we commend ourselves in every way: in great endurance; in troubles, hardships and distresses; in beatings, imprisonments and riots; in hard work, sleepless nights and hunger; in purity, understanding, patience and kindness; in the Holy Spirit and in sincere love; in truthful speech and in the power of God; with weapons of righteousness in the right hand and in the left; through glory and dishonor, bad report and good report; genuine, yet regarded as imposters; known, yet regarded as unknown; dying, and yet we live on; beaten, and yet not killed; sorrowful, yet always rejoicing; poor, yet making many rich; having nothing, and yet possessing everything" (2 Cor 6:3-10). These same attitudes Paul wisely nurtures in the younger men he trains, as a careful reading of the pastoral Epistles (1 and 2 Tim and Titus) quickly shows.

Meekness and gentleness (the last word might be rendered "forebearance"—the same term occurs in Phil 4:5), taken together, suggest that the person characterized by such virtues will be generous in his estimates of others, slow to take offense, well able to bear reproach, consistently above mere self-interest. By such meekness and gentleness, characteristics of Christ himself, Paul makes his appeal. But although the language is deeply ironical, it is not manipulative. In other words, Paul does not choose an ironical way of expressing himself for no other reason than to get himself out of a tough situation, taking irony in his hands as a flexible tool to shame his readers. The situation is far more serious than that. Paul's language is steeped in irony because the concrete situation he faces is ironical: the Corinthians are confusing meekness with weakness, gentleness with servility, and utterly ignoring the dominant characteristics of the Redeemer they claim to acknowledge as Lord. If the irony of Paul's language shames the Corinthians, it is because the Corinthians ought to be ashamed.

The level of the Corinthians' misunderstanding is pretty basic. Not only do they charge Paul with inconsistency—they say he is timid when present and bold when absent and writing letters—

they do not have a grasp of fundamental Christian virtues. The word rendered "timid" (2 Cor 10:1) is customarily translated "humble"; but they see in this humbleness not a grace but a weakness. To the devout and mature Christian, the word "humble" has positive connotations; in the mind of the Corinthians, it has negative overtones. Perhaps they adopt the same usage found in passages like the following from Xenophon (who ascribes the words to Socrates): "Moreover, nobility and dignity, self-abasement and servility, prudence and understanding, insolence and vulgarity, are reflected in the face and in the attitudes of the body whether still or in motion" (*Memorabilia* III.10.5). In this quotation, *self-abasement* (the same word rendered "timid" in 2 Cor 10:1) is coupled with servility; and together they stand over against nobility and dignity. This kind of humbleness is ignoble; it cringes from confrontation, sidles up to money and power and influence with the phony humility of an unprincipled politician, and acts forceful and strong only when it appears safe to do so. In short, the Corinthians said that "when Paul was there, he was a Uriah Heep, very humble and cringing and artful; and when he was away from them, he could pluck up his courage and be very resolute—on paper" (Plummer). Like many today, the Corinthians embraced an essentially triumphalistic understanding of greatness; and therefore they were ill prepared to consider an apostle great if he contravened that mold. The dimensions of their triumphalism will become increasingly apparent. What is already clear in this ironical prelude is that Paul responds not in terms of one-upmanship (for then he would be succumbing to the set of values espoused by the Corinthians) but in terms of the character and teaching of Christ. At stake is much more than party allegiance. The differences between Paul and the Corinthians turn on a clash of world views, on a fundamental disjunction of values, on profound disagreement regarding that which Christians should pursue.

B. The Appeal (v. 2)

After administering in the prelude a small dose of shock treatment by establishing a framework of values vastly different from those espoused by the Corinthians, Paul comes to the appeal itself. "I beg you" (2 Cor 10:2) is probably not greatly different in this context from "I appeal to you" (10:1): in both instances Paul puts himself in the place of a supplicant. The essence of the appeal is that he may not have to be as "bold" (as strong and severe) toward the Corinthians as he himself fully expects to be toward "some people." This is a gentle way of asking the Corinthians to change before it is too late. Once Paul arrives, he will have to take strong action: so in advance of his arrival he appeals to the Corinthians to change their patterns of conduct so that the threatened sternness may be avoided.

Four observations enable us to grasp the force of this appeal a little better. The *first* is that the precise nature of Paul's threat is progressively unveiled farther on in the text. A hint of what is to come crops up in 2 Cor 10:6: "And we will be ready to punish every act of disobedience, once your obedience is complete." The threat of apostolic chastisement is real (cf. 13:2); but it is up to the Corinthians to respond in such a way that Paul's visit will be "in love and with a gentle spirit" and not with "a whip" (1 Cor 4:21). Mistaking humility for servility, the Corinthians have accused him of being timid and weak in person; but unless certain unspecified things change in the church, they will discover just how stern the apostle Paul can be. Is that what they really want?

On the other hand, severity is not the face Paul would like to wear; for in the *second* place, Paul speaks of this severity as something he would "dare" to use, as if it is not his normal stance. More literally translated, verse 2 reads, "I beg you that when I come I may not have to display that confident boldness that I reckon *I shall dare to use* against some people." It is as if Paul recognizes that the prime purpose of the authority the Lord has entrusted to him is to build people up, not tear them down (2 Cor 10:8); and therefore if the situation he confronts demands the sterner course, he is uncomfortable and grieved. Doubtless he will take the remedial steps necessary; but far from flaunting his authority by rushing into disciplinary action, Paul envisions the prospect as a dare that cannot be avoided, not a challenge to be encountered with relish. His normal stance, his preferred posture before his converts, is "the meekness and gentleness of Christ."

The *third* thing to observe is that the "some people" whom Paul expects to confront are probably not the Corinthians

themselves, or some part of them. Paul does not say he expects
to be bold toward "some of you," but toward "some people." Not
only is there a good clue supporting this distinction in verse 6,
but the same distinction between the Corinthians and the "some
people" who constitute Paul's primary opposition at Corinth is
maintained throughout these chapters. For instance, in 2 Cor 12:11
it is clear that those addressed as "you Corinthians!" should have
defended Paul against the "super-apostles." But if this is the case,
then the force of Paul's appeal in 10:2 is that the Corinthians
themselves should take decisive action against the intruders, so
that Paul will not have to do so when he arrives. The Corinthians
are currently being duped by those whom Paul sees as dangerous
imposters; and Paul is therefore appealing to his converts to
exercise the discernment and discipline necessary to avoid a later
showdown between the apostolic "whip" and the intruders.

Fourth, the nature of the differences between Paul and the
interlopers now begins to surface. Paul expects he will have to
be bold toward "some people" who think that Paul lives "by the
standards of this world." The original might be literally
translated, "according to the flesh": i.e., Paul is accused of living
according to the flesh. What exactly does that mean?

In Pauline usage, "flesh" can refer to the physical substance
that drapes our bones. When compounded in an expression such
as "flesh and blood," it means something like "humanity" or
"human nature and mortality." But characteristically Paul uses
"flesh" to denote *fallen* human nature, man in sin and rebellion
against God, human beings mired in egocentricity and thereby
shoving God out to the periphery—if there is any place left for
him at all. But in the context of 2 Corinthians 10-13, it is unlikely
that Paul's opponents are accusing him of being essentially sinful
in the exercise of his apostleship. Rather, they are accusing him
of being an ineffective leader, given to excessive timidity, capable
of not more than third-rate preaching, and having too little
background in spiritual and visionary experiences to claim the
allegiance of the Corinthians. It is in this sense that Paul, in their
judgment, lives "according to the flesh" or "by the standards of
the world": he does not attain the high standards of spirituality
and leadership that they claim for themselves! He lives and
serves at the lowly level of this world, of flesh; they minister as
dynamic, spiritual leaders whose spiritual experiences attest

their superiority, and whose rhetoric demonstrates their God-
given graces.

Paul's language is gently ironic. He has spoken of the
confident boldness that he *reckons* he shall dare to use; now he
refers to these unnamed "some people" who *reckon* that Paul
lives by the standards of the world. At bottom is the question
of evaluation: Paul's opponents have evaluated him in a certain
light and dismissed him as inferior, and in the process they have
attempted to capture the allegiance of an entire church. Paul
evaluates them in a different light and insists they are imposters
(2 Cor 11:13-15) who are preaching another Jesus (v. 4), and
reckons he will dare to confront them with apostolic authority
when he finally arrives in Corinth. The pair of evaluations—
Paul's evaluation of the intruders, theirs of him—are fundamentally opposed.

But we must hasten to add that the differences between the
two evaluations do not spring from personal animosity or
pretentious pique. The root of the differences in evaluation is
the disjunction between the sets of criteria that the two parties
use. Doubtless the intruders think of themselves as gifted and
spiritual; but their criteria for assessing both themselves and
Paul have received their imprint from Judaizing Christianity,
from Hellenistic standards of rhetoric and leadership, and from
visionary enthusiasm. Paul responds by insisting in effect that
when these perspectives dominate, the resulting judgments are
sub-Christian. Judaizers will seek to prove their spiritual
superiority by making much of their racial and covenantal
pedigree (2 Cor 11:21a-22); sophists will judge a person's right
to lead by the competence or otherwise of his rhetoric (v. 6) and
by his ability to command a considerable income (v. 7); and
visionary enthusiasts will judge a potential leader by the number
and vividness of his alleged spiritual experiences (12:1-10). But
all such criteria, Paul perceives, depreciate Christ. If an essential
element of true spirituality is race, then it is not Christ's cross-
work and our consequent relationship to him that are determin-
ative; if standards of rhetoric and the ability to command a purse
are prime conditions for leadership in the church, then a servant
mentality is depreciated (even though Christ himself displayed
just such an attitude), and culturally bound standards of oratory
usurp the place of unchanging and culture-transcendent truth;

and if a display of the visionary's enthusiasm is the *sine qua non* for advanced leadership, not only is the church vulnerable to fraudulent claims, but the claimants themselves are likely to glory more and more in the esoteric, and not in the sufficiency of the grace of Christ.

The heart of the intruders' criteria is triumphalism; and in each case the criterion is grounded on something neither good nor evil in itself, but that is fundamentally evil when it serves to displace Christ or camouflage the true characteristics of spiritual leadership. In this sense, the criteria of evaluation proposed by the intruders were essentially non-Christian. Principially, they were pagan. The clash between Paul and the intruders was a clash of world views. Paul's world view was shaped by the gospel; theirs took its form from what was praised in the segments of society whose honor they cherished. Ironically, they were charging Paul with living according to worldly standards that were not up to their own level of spiritual worth, whereas in reality they had so misunderstood the gospel that their own values were truly worldly, according to the "flesh" in the customary Pauline sense—egocentric, sinful, rebellious against God and the revelation he had graciously provided.

This deep clash may seem strange to our society, for two reasons. First, we live in an age of deeply ingrained subjectivism. We have been taught to think that it is somehow wrong, even evil, to say that another's value system is false. The only absolute judgment widely endorsed by our society is that no absolute judgment is permissible. What suffers in this climate is truth— or, more precisely, the possibility of affirming the existence of any absolute truth. But conversely, if the gospel of Jesus Christ— all it provides and teaches and demands—is true, then that which opposes it is to that extent false. Truth is exclusive of error and falsehood. Paul does not bother to dispute anyone's prerogative to teach some system contrary to the gospel; but he does dispute their right to do so in the church, passing off the error as if it were gospel truth.

The second reason why our society may at first react negatively to the clash between Paul and the intruders is that, in addition to the problem of our unscrutinized subjectivism, we inhabit a place and time in history dominated by cultural diversity. In a sense, this is a very healthy thing, for it enlarges our horizons and in some cases increases our narrow tolerances. Indeed, at certain levels Paul himself was surely one of the most culturally flexible missionaries who ever lived. He writes, "To the Jews I became like a Jew, to win the Jews. To those under the law I became like one under the law (though I myself am not under the law), so as to win those under the law. To those not having the law I became like one not having the law (though I am not free from God's law but am under Christ's law), so as to win those not having the law. To the weak I became weak, to win the weak. I have become all things to all men so that by all possible means I might save some" (1 Cor 9:20-22). There lies extravagant and Christ-honoring flexibility.

Yet at the same time, regardless of the race and culture he was serving at the time, Paul recognized that the gospel itself is non-negotiable. In most societies relatively few individuals are willing to concede the moral limitations of their inherited values and learn to interpret them by an outside standard and if necessary curtail or abandon them. We find it easier to interpret the gospel in terms of our received culture than the other way around. Biblically speaking, however, all races and cultures are infected with sin. To the extent that the gospel clashes with any one of them, to that extent people who spring from such races and cultures and who profess faith in and allegiance to Jesus Christ must regard the good news of Jesus Christ as the controlling factor. The gospel will purify and transform any culture; or, more accurately, the gospel will purify and transform the people from any cultural heritage who bow unreservedly to Jesus Christ. By this means it will modify or eliminate many of the culturally transmitted values of those new Christians; and they in turn may in some measure influence their culture and society as salt exerts its influence in food (cf. Matt 5:13). But there will always be some who are controlled by a lightly "Christianized" version of their own culture: i.e., their controlling values spring from the inherited culture, even when such values are deeply pagan and not Christian. Christian language may be there; yet the control lies, not with the gospel, but with the pervasive values of the surrounding society and heritage. At that point Paul is inflexible.

As far as Christians are concerned, wherever there is a clash between a cherished inherited culture and the gospel of Jesus

Christ, it is the former that must give way and accept modification and transformation. Failure at this point calls in question one's allegiance to the gospel. Unreserved commitment to the priorities of the inherited culture, with select elements of Christianity being merely tacked on, brings with it Paul's inevitable conclusion that the Jesus being preached is "another Jesus," the gospel being proclaimed is a "different gospel," and those who proclaim such an Evangel are "deceitful workmen masquerading as apostles of Christ" (2 Cor 11:4,13). Moreover, those professing Christians who, like the Corinthians, show themselves to be profoundly sympathetic to this non-Christian orientation of values must at very least examine themselves again to see if they really are in the faith (13:5).

The full force of Paul's appeal to the Corinthians is now apparent. He begs them to reevaluate these intruders, for he does not want to be as bold toward them as he expects to be. In effect, he appeals to the Corinthians to return to the truth of the gospel and the teaching and example of Christ Jesus, and thereby see the contours of the intruders' doctrines for what they are. And meanwhile, Paul strongly insists that, contrary to the charge leveled against him by the intruders, he has never as a Christian lived "by the standards of the world" (2 Cor 10:2) nor fought his spiritual battle using "the weapons of the world" (v. 4).

C. Paul Denies that His Warfare Is Worldly (10:3,4a)

Paul concedes, of course, that the world is his sphere of activity; but that does not mean the world dictates the agenda, still less that it provides the tools for the job. "For though we live in the world," Paul writes, "we do not wage war as the world does" (2 Cor 10:3). And then, lest any reader has failed to grasp the force of what he has said, he reiterates, "The weapons we fight with are not the weapons of the world" (10:4a).

The NIV provides as accurate and free-flowing a translation of Paul's Greek idiom as might be hoped; but it is worth reflecting a little further on Paul's exact choice of words.

Two words deserve mention. First, the expression "we live," both in 2 Cor 10:2 and 10:3a, might more literally be rendered "we walk." The context of this word, both here and elsewhere in Paul, unambiguously shows that the apostle is thinking about something more than literal walking; and NIV's "we live" isn't bad. But perhaps it is a shade too passive: the force of Paul's "to walk" is not so narrow as "to live," but more like "to conduct one's life." Paul is not simply saying that the sphere of his existence is the world (though elsewhere he says this), but that the sphere where he conducts his life—where he lives out and discharges his responsibilities as an apostle—is this world. Yet even so, he insists, the weapons of his apostleship are not "of the world."

More importantly, Paul continues to use the word "flesh" or "fleshly" (see above). Paul conducts his life, literally, "in the flesh"; but he does not wage war according to the flesh, for the weapons of his warfare are not fleshly. We have already seen (2 Cor 10:2) that "flesh" can mean different things in Paul's usage: on the one hand, Paul can say Christians are no longer "in the flesh" (Rom 8:9 RSV), meaning that they no longer live by the biases of fallen, self-centered, and sinful human nature; and on the other hand, he admits he lives "in the flesh" (Gal 2:20 RSV), meaning that he lives in his body, in the physical world. Meanwhile, his opponents, as we have seen, have accused him of conducting his life according to the flesh (2 Cor 10:2), meaning that he falls short of the high, spiritual standards they claim for themselves. Thus, we have found three principal meanings for "flesh" so far:

1. sinful nature, man in rebellion against God—as in Rom 8:9
2. physical existence, body, the physical reality in which we still live—as in Gal 2:20
3. sub-standard spirituality, worldly or inferior standards, as understood by Paul's opponents, and charged against him— as in 2 Cor 10:2

The question is, What does Paul mean by his use of the term in its two occurrences in 10:3?

At one level, the question is easy to answer. In the first part of verse 3, Paul concedes that he conducts his life in the flesh, adopting meaning number 2. In the second part of verse 3, and the first part of verse 4, Paul insists he does not wage war according to the flesh—doubtless denying simultaneously any association with "flesh" according to meanings 1 and 3.

Yet at a deeper level, Paul's answer turns on a profound

grasp of eschatology, and introduces us to much that he will say to the Corinthians in the ensuing chapters. The New Testament writers, and not least Paul, understand that Jesus Christ, by his death, resurrection, ascension, and exaltation to the right hand of the majesty on high, has *already* introduced the Messianic kingdom long promised by the prophets and expected by the spiritually discerning among God's people. God has already rescued us from the dominion of darkness and brought us into the kingdom of the Son he loves (Col 1:13). At the same time, the kingdom has not dawned in its fullness: it will not be consummated until the Lord Jesus returns, when the whole creation will be renewed (Rom 8:19-21). In one sense therefore the church lives in a remarkable tension between what is "already" and what is "not yet": Christians already enjoy something of the kingdom's benefits—acquittal before God, possession of eternal life, the presence of the Holy Spirit as the downpayment of the final inheritance, the forgiveness of their sins, deep fellowship with other children of God, assurance that their risen Savior and Lord is already reigning with all of his Father's authority; yet Christians do *not yet* enjoy all the blessings that will one day be theirs—the abolition of death, the utter destruction of the power of sin, possession of resurrection bodies, free scope in a new heaven and a new earth, untarnished worship of the triune God, the bliss of undiluted love and unblemished holiness, the perfection of fellowship. Thus, New Testament eschatology is not a restricted focus on the last things, but includes the wonderful news that the last things have in certain respects already arrived. New Testament eschatology deals alternately with what is yet to come and with what has shatteringly, unexpectedly, magnificently arrived. In other words, New Testament eschatology is simultaneously futuristic and realized.

Failure to keep the balance breeds not only theological error but also moral and lifestyle problems of considerable severity. Over-emphasis on the futuristic aspects of eschatology, e.g., at the expense of the realized aspects, may foster unhealthy speculation regarding what God has not revealed, date-setting as to when Christ will return, a denial of the graces and benefits we have already received, and a depreciation of the importance of living together as Christians who constitute a kind of outpost of the new heaven and new earth. The opposite imbalance may prompt us to neglect the promises the Bible gives us regarding the future, to forget to live lives that look forward to and long for Christ's return, and to act as if the fullness of all Christ provided by his cross-work is already our due.

Unfortunately, throughout their recorded spiritual pilgrimage the Corinthians were prone to the second error, what some have called an over-realized eschatology. They rightly understood that the salvation Christ provides exalts poor sinners to become priests and kings; but they so emphasized these themes that they started to strut like peacocks, forgetting that until the parousia the church is also called to suffering witness (1 Cor 4:8-13). The Corinthians were inclined to stress their freedom in Christ (chap. 8); but they overlooked the fact that perfect freedom is possible only where there is perfect goodness—and the church has not yet reached that point. Freedom must therefore be expressed—and curbed!—by loving self-denial; but of this, the Corinthians had learned little. They were avid followers of spiritual gifts, and especially cherished those spiritual gifts that fed inflated egos (chaps. 12,14). Extravagant displays in their view prove how spiritual a person is, how much he has appropriated of all the blessings Jesus Christ has already provided. This pathetic spiritual one-upmanship was doubtless part of the cause of the party spirit that wracked the church (1:12); for somehow they had never learned to follow "the most excellent way" (12:31b-13:13), the way of self-giving love best exemplified in Jesus' earthly mission. In short, the Corinthians were quick to seize every emphasis in Christianity that spoke (or seemed to speak) of spiritual power, of exaltation with Christ, of freedom, of triumph, of victorious Christian living, of leadership, of religious success; but they neglected or suppressed those accents in Christianity that stressed meekness, servanthood, obedience, humility, and the need to follow Christ in his suffering if one is to follow him in his crown. They glimpsed what Christ had done, yet failed to contemplate what remains to be done; they understood that D-day had arrived, but mistook it for V-day. They loved Christian triumphalism, but they did not know how to live under the sign of the cross.

In this light, Paul's statement in 2 Corinthians 10:3 takes on new depths. Paul does not merely concede, but actually insists, that he lives in the world, that he conducts his life in the flesh; for the Corinthians were disposed to think of themselves as so spiritual that fleshly or worldly matters were of little concern to them. Apparently the intruders told many stories of their ecstatic and visionary experiences, and by this means greatly enhanced their credibility (see on 12:1-10); but if Paul in one remarkable vision does not know whether he is in the body or out of the body (12:2,3), he is quite certain that his normal sphere of operation is in the body, in the flesh, in the world. He may on occasion have deep desires to depart this world, quit the body and be with Christ (Phil 1:21-23); but he understands that remaining in this world and in the body is what enables him to be so fruitful a servant of the churches (1:24). At the same time, Paul insists with no less vehemence that, however much he may live in the world, his weapons are not of the world. If Paul is right on this point, then not only are his detractors wrong, but even their ability to distinguish spiritual realities is called into question. They judge Paul's weapons to be worldly, and he claims the opposite: the division between Paul and the intruders is not only clear-cut, but fundamental.

It thus becomes obvious that Paul does not see the issues before him as nothing more than a personality conflict, an unpleasant and dirty little power grab. The orientation of the triumphalists' entire value system is inverted: they claim to be spiritual in precisely those areas where Paul claims he is in the world, and they accuse Paul of being worldly in precisely those areas where Paul insists his weapons are spiritual! This entails a disturbingly distorted eschatology: the intruders foster an over-realized eschatology when they overlook the elementary truth that Christians still conduct their lives in the world. Yet when it comes to genuine spiritual discernment, the intruders show themselves to be virtually bankrupt as they assess Paul's gifts by the fleeting standards of contemporary rhetoric or seek to establish a preacher's credentials by the size of his following or the wealth in his wallet.

We may marvel that professing Christians—leaders, at that—can be so deeply wrong, so profoundly misguided. But before we think of modern parallels, and reflect on how to apply Paul's defense to our own day, perhaps we should first take note of his counter claim.

D. Paul's Specifications of the Nature and Purpose of His Weapons (10:4b, 5)

Not only does 2 Corinthians 10:4a reiterate and reinforce verse 3, it also prepares for Paul's positive claim: accusations to the contrary, Paul's weapons "have divine power to demolish strongholds." By this short sentence Paul makes two crucial statements. He specifies the nature of his weapons, and he stipulates their purpose. Verse 5 is further elaboration of these points.

Paul's weapons "have divine power." The Greek is slightly ambiguous,[1] but the main point is clear: Paul's weapons are powerful because they are related to God. Far from being fleshly or of the world, they are spiritual, and therefore they have power (Lietzmann).

The contrast Paul is drawing must not be overlooked. He is not comparing, say, tanks, rifles, and missiles with prayer, fasting, and preaching. The fleshly or worldly side of the contrast depends on the interpretation of 2 Corinthians 3-4a: worldly weapons in this context are the kinds of tools of the trade relished by the intruders: human ingenuity, rhetoric, showmanship, a certain splashiness and forwardness in spiritual pretensions, charm, powerful personal charisma. Such weapons they will not find in Paul's arsenal, so they think him inferior; but Paul responds by openly disavowing such weapons. He would not want to defend himself on that score, for his weapons are of an entirely different sort. They are spiritual weapons, and they are divinely powerful (or powerful in God's perspective or for his service).

But what can Paul's weapons do? If we agree they are

---

1. Greek *dynata tō theō* could be understood in one of four ways: (1) instrumental dative: Paul's weapons are "made powerful by God"; (2) Hebraism: Paul's weapons are "divinely powerful" or "supernaturally powerful"; (3) dative of respect: Paul's weapons are "powerful in God's perspective"; (4) dative of advantage: Paul's weapons are "powerful for God," i.e., for God's service. The first two options are conceptually very close, and NIV presupposes one or the other. But all four options in some way relate the weapons and their power to God.

powerful, how is their power manifest? That brings us to the second element in Paul's statement. His weapons, he claims, have power "to demolish strongholds." Paul's symbolism calls to mind a classic form of warfare in the ancient world. A prosperous city would not only build a stout wall for its security, but somewhere inside the wall it might also build a stronghold—i.e., a massively fortified tower that could be defended by relatively few soldiers. Even if the walls of the city were breached by the enemy, the defending forces could retreat to the stronghold and make a final defense there. Once the stronghold was taken, the battle was over. Extolling wisdom, Proverbs 21:22 reads, "A wise man attacks the city of the mighty and pulls down the stronghold in which they trust." Using just such language, Paul claims his weapons have divine power "to demolish strongholds."

What does this mean in nonmetaphorical language? Paul unpacks his metaphor in the next sentence. He continues the theme of demolition, but changes the object: "We demolish arguments and every pretension that sets itself up against the knowledge of God." The word translated "arguments" might be rendered "thoughts" or "plans." It is cognate with a term Paul uses elsewhere with a very similar meaning. For instance, Paul describes the progressive deterioration of the human race when he says that although people once knew God, "they neither glorified him as God nor gave thanks to him, but their *thinking* became futile and their foolish hearts were darkened" (Rom 1:21). "The Lord knows that the *thoughts* of the wise are futile" (1 Cor 3:20). Again, Paul tells believers to "do everything without complaining or *arguing*" (Phil 2:14). When he tells us that his weapons demolish *arguments*, therefore, he does not simply mean that he can out-debate any opponent and drive him shamefaced from the stage. He means something far more: his weapons destroy the way people think, demolish their sinful thought patterns, the mental structures by which they live their lives in rebellion against God. In his own words, his spiritual weapons tear down "every pretension that sets itself up against the knowledge of God" (v. 5).

What Paul has in mind is related to the very fountainhead of sin in our lives. "Every pretension that sets itself up against the knowledge of God" embraces every arrogant claim, every haughty thought, every proud act that forms a barrier to the knowledge of the living God. We were created dependent creatures; the heart of sin is rebellion against God, a pervasive attitude that wants above all to be independent of God. This willful drive for independence is the root of sin, the core evil that rightly attracts the wrath of God. We do "not think it worthwhile to retain the knowledge of God" (Rom 1:28; cf. vv. 18-32). Instead we erect pretensions to shut out the knowledge of God. We claim intellectual doubt, we appeal to the arguments of sophistry and skepticism, we display a supercilious and condescending cynicism; or we merely remain aloof and distant, claiming an intellectual independence that loves to debate theology without ever bending the knee in adoring worship. But we have not adequately weighed the catastrophic entailment. Because we have shielded ourselves from the knowledge of God, God has given us over to a depraved mind. Emptied of the knowledge of God, we become filled not only with ourselves, but "with every kind of wickedness, evil, greed and depravity." We become "full of envy, murder, strife, deceit and malice." We degenerate until we are "gossips, slanderers, God-haters, insolent, arrogant and boastful." We "invent ways of doing evil," disobey our parents and become "senseless, faithless, heartless, ruthless." Worse, although we know "God's righteous decree that those who do such things deserve death," we "not only continue to do those very things but also approve those who practice them" (Rom 1:28-32).

This is why "every pretension that sets itself up against the knowledge of God" is so desperately serious, and deeply tied in to the fountainhead of sin in our lives. We cannot know God from a position of arrogance and cynicism; for not only are such attitudes fundamentally antithetical to our creaturely dependence, they are also foundationally opposed to the only knowledge of God open to poor sinners, viz., Jesus Christ crucified.

That is the heart of the issue; and it is something Paul had already taught the Corinthians. He had earlier written to them: "For since in the wisdom of God the world through its wisdom did not know him, God was pleased through the foolishness of what was preached to save those who believe. Jews demand miraculous signs and Greeks look for wisdom, but *we preach Christ crucified,* a stumbling block to Jews and foolishness to

Gentiles" (1 Cor 1:21-23). On the whole, Jews expected a triumphant Messiah who would scatter the forces of Rome and establish afresh the independence and supremacy of Israel. A Messiah who had to die the ignominious death of a shamed criminal could scarcely be thought powerful enough to take on Rome or worthy enough to be followed. Even the accounts of his resurrection could not wipe out the stigma of his self-abasement; so Christ crucified was a stumbling block. But Gentiles by and large adhered to patterns of religion that advocated self-improvement in various ways. Salvation gained by another's death was strange, even foolish; one might almost question whether such a putative savior could be of any value if he so lacked integrity and skill that he died an ignoble death.

Paul might have gone on with his illustration, for the notion of Christ crucified is foundationally offensive. The Buddhist believes he can purify himself; the Hindu anticipates countless cycles of reincarnation as he plods upward toward Nirvana; the Muslim insists that God is so powerful he may simply forgive without reference to any atoning sacrifice; the religiously superstitious may treat a crucifix as if it were a talisman, a magical trinket to ward off misfortune and disaster; the religiously sophisticated may busily debate theories of the atonement and the nature of the resurrection body, but exhibit little trust in Messiah and his cross-work. To one and all, Christ crucified may still be a stumbling block or foolishness; "but to those whom God has called, both Jews and Greeks, Christ the power of God and the wisdom of God" (1 Cor 1:24).

The problem Paul confronts now stands out starkly. By God's design at creation, we are dependent beings whose purpose is to know and worship and trust God, and the root of our sin is rebellion against that wise design. By God's plan of redemption, there is hope of forgiveness and life only to those who bow at the cross and receive forgiveness of sin and the person of the Spirit as free gifts of grace. By contrast, triumphalists, self-sufficient types, unbroken people who would not or could not think of bending the knee, dismiss this saving plan as religious camp or blatant nonsense. The problem is one: human pride, unwilling to learn or repent, rushes to erect new pretensions against the knowledge of God, new arguments from an artificial position of intellectual strength to dismiss "mere Christianity" or to write it off as "the opiate of the people." Worse, these inglorious pretensions often adopt the language and ritual of biblical Christianity and systematically strip away its power by investing it with new meaning, until ultimately another Jesus is being preached (cf. 2 Cor 11:4). Such arguments and pretensions as these are what Paul's spiritual weaponry has the power to demolish. Now Paul expands the language of warfare: his weapons not only demolish these mental strongholds, they are powerful enough to "take captive every thought to make it obedient to Christ" (2 Cor 10:5). The picture is of a military expedition into enemy territory, an expedition so effective that every plan of the enemy is thwarted, every scheme foiled, every counter-offensive beaten. More: these designs and schemes of sinful men are captured by Christ and brought under a new authority. The idea in this verse is not simply that Christ so takes hold of people that they think holy thoughts (though that is true: cf. Phil 4:8), but that their mental structures, their plans and schemes, are taken over and transformed as they come into a new allegiance. Using his spiritual weapons Paul takes captive every scheme (as the same word is translated in 2:11), every mind (as it is rendered in 2 Cor 11:13), and makes it obedient to Christ.

Paul's point in making this extraordinary statement appears to be threefold. *First*, it highlights the nature of the conflict. If the Christian's weapons are essentially spiritual, so also is the conflict—a point Paul makes elsewhere when he writes that our struggle is not against "flesh and blood" (i.e., mortal man) but against a vast array of spiritual enemies (Eph 6:12). *Second*, Paul is insisting that his weapons are producing results. The astonishing thing about Paul's preaching of the gospel in the first century is that although his message was a stumblingblock to Jews and nonsense to Gentiles, both Jews and Gentiles were being converted. The gospel may be a scandal to some and folly to others, but it is powerful enough to capture representatives of this proud and unregenerate race. Many who cherish their "freedom" and dismiss the crucified Christ with scorn come in time to embrace his lordship, cherish his cross, abandon self-promotion, and exchange it for self-denial and obedience.

There is a *third* point, made clear by the context. Since Paul is setting his spiritual and powerful weapons over against the claims to leadership advanced by the intruders, he is not only clarifying the nature and purpose of his own weapons, but he is implicitly exposing the nature and futility of theirs for the conflict at hand. True, their arguments, rhetoric, boasts, methods, claims to ecstatic experience, and the like may win a following, sweep a church, win a certain fame; but can they transform people? Paul's weapons have divine power to demolish the convictions and pretensions of those who set themselves and their self-declared "autonomous" reason against the truth of God, and to capture the minds and opinions of these one-time rebels: can the false apostles claim the same thing for their weapons? Indeed, Paul almost hints that their weapons are not only powerless for the task at hand, but that they actually constitute part of the problem, part of the rebellious mental world of sinful man, who wants to be the self-sufficient center of the universe instead of bowing to God and his true revelation. The intruders may be good at seducing a church and introducing another gospel; but are they any good at breaking down arrogant human beings and bringing them to the refuge of the cross? That this is included in Paul's protest is confirmed a few verses later when, as we shall see, he points out that his proclamation of the gospel did extend, with success, as far as Corinth (2 Cor 10:13-15a)—which is why the Corinthians themselves are Christians! What similar credentials can the intruders advance?

What are Paul's spiritual weapons, these weapons with such magnificent power? We could deduce most of them from these chapters; but Paul himself provides a convenient list in Ephesians 6:13-18, where he exhorts believers to "put on the full armor of God." Using the extended metaphor of the equipment worn and carried by a common Roman foot soldier, Paul lists the essential elements of the Christian's weaponry:[2] the truth of the gospel, righteousness, readiness and boldness borne of a deep grasp of the gospel of peace, faith, salvation itself, the Word of God, and vigilant prayer.

These are Paul's powerful weapons! Not one depends on

2. In Paul's extended metaphor of Eph 6:14-17, it is important to recognize that the genitives are epexegetical. Just as in the expression "the city of Jerusalem" the city *is* Jerusalem, so also in the expression "the breastplate of righteousness" the breastplate *is* righteousness.

gimmickry, still less on proud human pretensions. True, Paul is prepared to use all legitimate means to save some (1 Cor 9:22), just as today we may legitimately use computers, television, and printing presses. But ultimately Paul's understanding of the nature of his effective, spiritual weaponry (as opposed to a few external means) holds true for our day as it did for his.

We are now better situated to think more closely about how this text speaks to contemporary evangelicalism, especially Western evangelicalism. At the risk of considerable oversimplification, we may divide that evangelicalism into two groups. *Group One* is relatively placid. It goes through the accepted motions, is basically faithful (esp. in formal matters), but knows little of the power of the gospel. *Group Two* is aggressive, active, triumphalistic. Not a little of the American can-do mentality is mixed in with it. It gains a substantial hearing, expects to see victory and joy in its followers, and harnesses enormous energy and many skills to the task of promoting its understanding of the gospel.

This is quite clearly a caricature. There are many Christians who fit neither group. Nevertheless the model embraces large blocks of Western Christianity, and it is worth pausing to ask what impact the text ought to make on such groups.

In its most virulent forms, Group Two suffers from an overrealized eschatology—just as the Corinthians did. Group Two Christians so magnify the many promises of God for health, prosperity, and victory that they reflect little on what the Bible also says about suffering, persecution, steadfastness in defeat, and death. Deeply, if unwittingly, influenced by the materialism around us and by the American ideal of the classic success story, they transfer such models into the church; and, ignorant of both church history and the balance of Scripture, they lay themselves open to teachers whose grasp of the biblical gospel is badly skewed. I shall say more about these things later and provide more concrete examples; but already, even from the verses at hand (esp. 2 Cor 10:3-5), it is important to call attention to such tragic features as self-promotion in Christian leadership, and to a profound dependence on psychological manipulation, mass circulation of glib how-to formulas for instant spiritual maturity and material prosperity, and a frank appeal to endless self-interest, that such features as principial daily death to self-interest (= taking up one's cross and following the Lord Jesus Christ), maturity stimulated by suffering (= God's grace is made perfect in weakness), and the abolition of doubtful, manipulative techniques (= rejection of a style of proclamation that is nothing more than wise and persuasive words, 1 Cor 2:4) are ignored or buried in the deluge of success stories.

Meanwhile, Group One avoids the triumphalism of Group Two and sometimes criticizes Group Two; but instead of wielding Paul's powerful, divine weapons, the members of this camp go through formal motions of religion, adhere to orthodox confessions, expect little of real blessing or joy in the Lord, and experience even less of the same.

The result is that both Group One and Group Two, if for very different reasons, shy away from the weapons Paul recommends, and to the extent that we belong to either group, we discover as a result, if we are honest in our self-criticism, that our weapons lack divine power to demolish the strongholds that interest Paul. Why is there a rising number of "evangelicals" without a corresponding swell of God-centered worship, repentance, unfeigned faith, humility, righteousness? Of course, there are many exceptions, many individual Christians who have truly been transformed by the grace of God; but their numbers fall so far short of those who think of themselves as evangelical Christians that we must ask if some forms of evangelicalism are falling progressively out of step with the Scriptures on such points as these.

I shall cast the matter in a more positive light. One of the things we badly need in Western Christianity is a return to the balance of Paul. On the one hand, we must recognize we live in the world: some eschatological blessings will ordinarily be withheld from us until the consummation. At the same time, although the weapons for spiritual warfare God has given us are divinely powerful, they are bound up with the very nature of this "foolish" gospel we proclaim. Argue a skeptic into a corner, and you will not take his mind captive for Christ; but pray for him, proclaim the gospel to him, live out the gospel of peace, walk righteously by faith until he senses your ultimate allegiance and citizenship are vastly different from his own, and you may discover that the power of truth, the convicting and regenerating work of the Holy Spirit, and the glories of Christ Jesus shatter his reasons and demolish his arguments until you take captive his mind and heart to make them obedient to Christ. The result will be a life transformed. Gone will be the principial egocentricity, the self-proclaimed independence. Replacing it will be a cheerful and devoted submission to the lordship of Christ. Only the weapons Paul advocates are sufficient to accomplish so stupendous a task. In the spiritual arena a successful campaign can be fought only when worldly weapons are self-consciously abandoned, and all our reliance is firmly set on the spiritual weapons, which alone have divine power to demolish the strongholds where rebel minds cling to idolatrous, God-rejecting self-sufficiency and manufacture new forms of entrenched evil. Paul sounds a call to return to biblical basics.

E. Paul's Promise of Discipline Against the Troublemakers—A Promise Predicated on an Obedient Church (10:6)

Paul's appeal (2 Cor 10:2) comes full circle. He has begged the church to take the kind of action necessary to silence the "some people" who have been accusing him of worldliness; and now he affirms his own willingness "to punish every act of disobedience" once the church has taken its preliminary step of obedience.

This verse is often misunderstood. Some have taken it to mean that once the Corinthians have repented and turned in obedience to Paul and his doctrine, he will then descend on them with punishment for their past acts of disobedience. This is not very realistic. For a start, such an interpretation makes Paul's promise of punishment a *dis*incentive to repentance: he will chastise them as soon as they toe the line! Moreover, it leaves Paul in the perilous position of presenting himself yet again as weak and unimpressive in person: he cannot even exercise a little discipline until the Corinthians have already straightened out their own course.

What Paul is really saying is that he will be ready to punish every act of disobedience *by the interlopers and by any who persist in following them,* once the church as a whole has brought its own obedience to perfection by exercising the kind of discipline hitherto conspicuous by its absence.

This does not mean Paul is afraid to act unilaterally, or is powerless to do so. Indeed, later on he uses very strong language to describe his personal readiness to discipline the entire church (2 Cor 13:1-3,10); but here his appeal is for obedient faith by the church, so that his special apostolic sanctions (the nature of which I shall discuss later) will have to be applied only to a small minority, and in conjunction with the church's discipline. In short, he is writing to see if the Corinthians "would stand the test and be obedient in everything" (2:15), not only because his severity is a weapon of last resort, but also to give every possible opportunity for the Corinthians to take responsible steps themselves. That is the burden of Paul's appeal, as it was in an earlier disciplinary matter (cf. 1 Cor 5:1-10). This accurately reflects the high value Paul places on disciplinary action *taken by the church as a whole;* for not only will such corporate action breed corporate maturity, but also this is the only kind of ecclesiastical action with genuine potency. Only if the body as a whole makes the offenders feel the sting of reproach and the shame of loving but firm ostracism will the step prove effective. Paul therefore begs (2 Cor 10:2) the Corinthian believers to take these hard decisions and assures the church that in the wake of their obedience he himself will add apostolic punishment to continuing offenders who trouble the church by maligning not only the apostle but his gospel.

What Paul appeals for is obedient faith. The Corinthians now face a clear-cut choice, presented by an apostle who makes his begging appeal by the meekness and gentleness of Christ. Either they will continue in disobedience, or they will exercise church discipline. Full-orbed obedient faith is not purely private and pietistic; it entails the responsibilities of corporate discipline. The church that forgets or neglects this lesson will sooner or later become much more of a "mixed company" than it has any right to be. Its self-proclaimed breadth and sophistication may be nothing more than an indicator of its disobedience.

3

The Ugliness of Spiritual One-upmanship
How Not to Boast in the Lord

2 Corinthians 10:7-18

⁷ You are looking only on the surface of things. If anyone is confident that he belongs to Christ, he should consider again that we belong to Christ just as much as he. ⁸ For even if I boast somewhat freely about the authority the Lord gave us for building you up rather than pulling you down, I will not be ashamed of it. ⁹ I do not want to seem to be trying to frighten you with my letters. ¹⁰ For some say, "His letters are weighty and forceful, but in person he is unimpressive and his speaking amounts to nothing." ¹¹ Such people should realize that what we are in our letters when we are absent, we will be in our actions when we are present.

¹² We do not dare to classify or compare ourselves with some who commend themselves. When they measure themselves by themselves and compare themselves with themselves, they are not wise. ¹³ We, however, will not boast beyond proper limits, but will confine our boasting to the field God has assigned to us, a field that reaches even to you. ¹⁴ We are not going too far in our boasting, as would be the case if we had not come to you, for we did get as far as you with the gospel of Christ. ¹⁵ Neither do we go beyond our limits by boasting

of work done by others. Our hope is that, as your
faith continues to grow, our area of activity among
you will greatly expand, [16] so that we can preach
the gospel in the regions beyond you. For we do not
want to boast about work already done in another
man's territory. [17] But, "Let him who boasts boast
in the Lord." [18] For it is not the one who commends
himself who is approved, but the one whom the
Lord commends.

The theme of boasting dominates the text
from here to the end of 2 Corinthians 12:10. Small wonder: Paul,
as we have seen, is confronting intruders in the Corinthian
assembly, leaders who advance their prestige and enhance their
personal reputations by adopting worldly postures on a wide
range of matters. More accurately, they not only adopt worldly
postures, they treat these like Christian virtues, making it
difficult for the spiritually immature Corinthians to resist the
seduction. Near the heart of their style of leadership is a kind
of triumphalistic self-promotion that Paul detests; but he finds
himself in the awkward position of needing to present his own
credentials as forcefully as possible—and what is this but
another form of the boasting he despises?

The way Paul handles this extraordinarily difficult situation
is to sidle up to his topic. He will not actually embark on his
list of boasts until the last half of 2 Corinthians 11. First he must
dispense with various false charges, dispel certain misconcep-
tions and set out a truly Christian framework which, if properly
grasped, already sentences triumphalism to its doom.

A. The Ugly Problem and Paul's Response (10:7-11)

1. Looking at the facts (10:7a). The Greek text in the first
line of verse 7 is a trifle ambiguous. It could be taken one of
three ways. First, it might be a question, as in the King James
Version: "Do ye look on things after the outward appearance?"—
i.e., "Do you see (only) what is material or fleshly?" There is little
to commend this rendering; for although it suits the context of
the preceding paragraph, it does not easily link up with what
follows. Second, the sentence might be rendered as in the NIV:

"You are looking only on the surface of things." This would mean Paul is not discouraging the Corinthians from checking credentials, but charging them with using superficial and worldly criteria. This can be shown to make a lot of sense in the context. Yet there are two weaknesses to this interpretation that encourage us, on balance, to adopt a third rendering: (i) the verb used is normally in the imperative in Paul: and (ii) there is nothing in the terms used here to suggest that what the Corinthians are looking at is worldly or superficial. These considerations prompt us to adopt the translation of the NIV footnote: "Look at the obvious facts."

This suits the context exactly. Paul has been appealing to the Corinthians to clean up their church, to inject obedience into their faith. Such obedience would be demonstrated by the disciplinary action they are exhorted to take against the interlopers. But to take such steps, they will have to make some judgments as to whether Paul or the intruders are to be believed and followed. All along, the Corinthians have been under the seductive influence of the false apostles. If they are to break free from their guile and reestablish truly Christian priorities, the Corinthian believers will have to change their evaluations, not least their evaluations of Paul. That is why the apostle now tells them, "Look at the obvious facts"—and then proceeds to offer obvious answers to some of the most scurrilous charges against him.

All this presupposes that a local church has the responsibility to make judgments; but the judgments should be based, not on powerful personalities capable of leading a church astray by the sheer energy of their will and personal attractiveness, but by more objective criteria, by obvious facts, by standards of Christian maturity. Some of these facts and standards emerge in the rest of 2 Corinthians 10; others appear in subsequent sections (e.g., 11:23-28; 12:9,10,12-15; 13:5,6). This balance is something every church must constantly seek to attain. Some churches and some Christians are very harsh in their judgments of others. Their criteria for judging leave something to be desired. Other churches and Christians, repulsed by what they feel is narrow sectarianism, advocate the broadest tolerance, and remind everyone that Jesus taught, "Do not judge, or you too will be judged" (Matt 7:l). But they overlook the fact that by adopting this stance they are passing judgment on those whom they judge to judge too harshly! Moreover, Jesus' teaching is in reality a condemnation of judgmentalism, not an invitation to vacuous moral indecision; for he himself elsewhere insists, "Stop judging by mere appearances, and make a right judgment" (John 7:24).

It is quite impossible for either an individual or a church to make no judgments; for even the failure to make decisions is in fact a decision based on the implicit assumption that the circumstances are not weighty enough to force a judgment. If the Corinthian church in the situation before us decided to make no judgments, it would in fact be deciding to disobey the apostle. Neither an individual Christian nor a church can avoid responsibility by refusing to make judgments; for that very refusal is already a judgment, an evaluation of commitments, strategies, priorities, and competing truth claims.

What this means is that since we cannot avoid making judgments we had better commit ourselves to making good ones. We will eschew cheap judgmentalism, remembering that we ourselves are at best poor sinners saved by grace. We will constantly ask God for the grace and wisdom to avoid decisions based on flattery, personal prejudice or pique, faulty understanding of Scripture, carelessness, or other impure or lazy motives. Instead, we will want to be fair and just, to test everything by Scripture maturely understood, to judge evenhandedly and on the basis of the immutables of the gospel of Jesus Christ and its practical entailments. If the Corinthians had practiced such distinctively Christian discernment and judging, they would not now be in the position of having to make extraordinarily painful and difficult decisions. They would not have been deceived by the interlopers in the first place, and would not now be called on to remove them. Life is built up of a series of interlocking decisions. Failure at a relatively easy level frequently returns to haunt us.

2. Putting Paul down (10:7b-11). If these verses provide Paul's response to some specific charges made by the interlopers, they also show what two of those charges were.

First, the false apostles claimed to belong to Christ in some special sense (10:7b). Exactly what this special sense consisted in is difficult to determine at this distance. It cannot simply mean that the opponents claimed to be Christians (which is the meaning "belonging to Christ" has in 1 Cor 15:23), for all the Corinthian believers would cheerfully claim the same thing, and therefore to belong to Christ in this sense would not constitute any distinctive claim to leadership in the Christian community. Moreover, as harsh as the intruders seem to be toward Paul, there is little evidence that they went so far as to say Paul was not even a Christian. Some scholars have therefore suggested that these opponents claimed to belong to the "Christ-party" mentioned in 1 Corinthians 1:12. But if that were so, why would Paul respond that he belongs to Christ as much as anyone else? The Paul who denounced the schismatic spirit in 1 Corinthians 1 would not likely now be claiming to belong to one of those parties himself. Moreover, judging by the kind of support the false apostles enjoyed in the entire Corinthian assembly, it appears they were not identified exclusively with some subgroup in the assembly. In other words, although "belonging to Christ" in 1 Corinthians 15:23 means something like "being a Christian," and in 1 Corinthians 1:12 means something like "belonging to some self-proclaimed 'Christ-party' (as opposed to a 'Peter-party' or 'Paul-party' or 'Apollos-party')," neither meaning fits the context in 2 Corinthians 10:7.

As a result, some modern writers have put forward various other explanations of doubtful worth. But perhaps the true explanation is a rather subtle one. The intruders quite clearly claimed to be "servants of Christ" in some special sense (see comments on 2 Cor. 11:23), and perhaps also "apostles of Christ" (11:13) and "servants of righteousness." Their claim to belong to Christ was therefore probably of a piece with the many other labels they proudly sported as means to win the Corinthians' confidence. As Barrett suggests, the opponents would need only say, with the right sort of inflection and tilt of the head, "I am Christ's man"—and they would simultaneously be claiming something for themselves and hinting that Paul was *not* Christ's man, that he did not belong to Christ in exactly the same way. The person who makes such a claim, and not Paul, is the authentic and authoritative apostle. Perhaps the proud boasts of these intruders held other connotations now lost to us: e.g., some of these leaders may have actually known the historical Jesus in the days of his flesh, may have claimed to know the resurrected Christ with special, mystical intimacy (cf. 12:1-10), or have even hinted that if Paul claimed to be their equal, his very standing as a Christian could be called into question. But these possibilities are not certain, and not central. What is clear is that Paul was presented to the Corinthians as someone who did not belong to Christ in the superior way claimed by the false apostles.

They had a *second* way of putting Paul down: they charged him with inconsistency, especially in the contrast between his powerful letters and his unimpressive personal presence. "His letters are weighty and forceful," they[1] said, "but in person he is unimpressive and his speaking amounts to nothing" (2 Cor. 10:10). In one sense, of course, they were right: charges that sting, even when false, usually approximate the truth in certain respects, or else they would have no credibility. Certainly some of Paul's letters were weighty, a point later recognized by Scripture itself (cf. 2 Pet 3:16). The Corinthian believers, as we have seen, had already received at least three letters from Paul. The second of these is our 1 Corinthians—a "forceful" letter if ever there was one; and the third, though effective, was painful and severe (cf. 2 Cor 2:4; 7:8-13). But when Paul showed up in person, he conveyed no personal aura or charisma, and his speaking invited contempt. In part, this doubtless sprang from the self-acknowledged deficiencies in his training (11:6); but at a deeper level, it sprang from his own commitment to eschew gimmickry and persuasive eloquence (1 Cor 1:17; 2:1-5) in order that the faith of his converts might rest, neither on his personality nor on his rhetoric, but on the power of God.

Whatever Paul's reasons, his opponents interpreted the facts in the worst possible light, and charged him with being guilty of a miserable inconsistency. Indeed, the charge is more cutting than first meets the eye; for it is not just that Paul's letters and Paul's presence prove inconsistent, but that *only* the letters are

---

1. There is a difficult variant here, *phēsin* or *phasin* but probably the singular is correct: lit. "someone says" or "he says" rather than "they say" or some say." But this singular may refer either to a specific opponent, a ringleader of the intruders, or may be a device common in the Greek diatribe, in which a writer might say, referring to his opponent in debate, "Someone will say . . ."— in which case the NIV's plural, though paraphrastic, is a close modern equivalent.

impressive. There is an implicit charge of duplicity, of phony boldness: he manages to present a brave front by using his gifted pen, but when Paul the man is assessed he turns out to be far inferior to his writings. It was easy to make the charge credible among those who felt that true Christian leadership should be impressive, bold, visionary, triumphalistic, and characterized by signs and rhetoric. All the opponents had to do was confuse meekness with weakness, and so adhere to the temporary standards of polished rhetoric (not to truth, integrity, or righteousness!) that they could brand "his artless preaching as being unworthy of the attention of educated Greeks" (Wilson).

How easily do we stoop to one-upmanship! When we hear stories of some interchange, does the narrator slant his account in such a way as to appear to have come out on top? Are we any different when we tell personal stories whose tone and shading constantly cry out, "I sure told them where to step off!" We may be so enamoured of the inner ring syndrome that we long to be inside some special group and are prepared to sacrifice Christian integrity in order to win that group's approval. It is arguable, e.g., that the most divisive aspects of certain forms of the charismatic movement, and of certain aspects of Reformed theology, are the strong in/out stances they project. You are either in (agreeing with them, participating with them, defending them, depreciating others) or out (disagreeing with them, not participating with them, sometimes attacking them, consolidating a flank with others against them). The polarization can become strong enough that the out group begins to constitute its own in mentality, based on antipathy to the opposing group. This is the stuff of schism.

Of course, I am not naively suggesting that theological distinctions are of little or no importance. I am referring rather to attitude. A charismatic, a Baptist, or a Reformed theologian who presses his case humbly, gently, prayerfully, may be completely innocent of this inner ring mentality. Indeed, it may be in some cases that the only inner ring to poison relationships is found in the closing ranks of the opposing majority who are threatened by the challenge. Rarely, however, is all the fault on one side; and the doctrinal questions are easily intermingled with a great deal of emotional one-upmanship unseemly among brothers in Christ. Certainly the Corinthian interlopers joined their doctrinal aberrations (see comments on 11:4) with a proud triumphalism designed to promote themselves into some inner circle of elite elect, accomplished in part by putting Paul down. And surely our one-upmanship is not more meritorious when we engage in the same exercise for no doctrinal reason whatsoever—when we condescendingly refer to fellow believers whose theological structures are similar to our own and (invariably in their absence) talk about them in ways so sophisticated that although we have not libeled them we have decisively demeaned them and put them down.

3. Paul's defense (10:7b-11). Paul answers this pair of charges, and the attitudes underlying them, by making three points.

First, he insists he belongs to Christ no less than do his opponents: "If anyone is confident that he belongs to Christ, he should consider again that we belong to Christ just as much as he" (2 Cor 10:7b). The word "again" probably means that such a person should take another look at himself, and on the basis of the fresh information conclude that the apostle Paul belongs to Christ no less than he.[2] Whatever "belonging to Christ means," Paul "argues that the right to make a subjective claim based on personal conviction cannot fairly be granted to his opponents and yet denied him" (Harris).

Yet doubtless there is a deeper principle at stake, even if it does not explicitly surface. After all, Paul is not at this point arguing that he is intrinsically superior to the others, or that he belongs to Christ more than they do. Later on when he is forced to talk about his visions (2 Cor 12:1-10), he refers to himself not as a great apostle entrusted with special revelations, but as "a man in Christ" (v. 2), a mere Christian, who was graciously accorded an ineffable vision. Even when he is forced to defend himself or when he argues there are different levels of Christian maturity and different roles to play in the body, he is careful not to erect any fences that might enclose inner-ring groups of Christians. Different roles, different gifts, different levels of maturity and understanding—yes; categorically different sorts of Christians, never!

---

2. I take *palin* ("again") to refer to the reflexive *heautō* (lit. "if anyone is confident in himself" or "with regard to himself").

Many of the children of God are far better than we are, and the worst one in his family has some points in which he is better than we are. I feel, sometimes, as though I would give my eyes to be as sure of heaven as the most obscure and the least in all the family of God; and I think that such times may come to some of you if you imagine yourselves to be so great and good. You strong cattle, that push with horn and with shoulder, and that drive back the weak ones, the Lord may say to you, "Get you gone; you belong not to me, for my people are not thus rough and boastful—not thus proud and haughty; but I look to the man who is humble, to him who has a contrite spirit, and who trembles at my Word."

Did you ever try to pray to God under the influence of a consciousness of possessing the higher life? Did you ever try to pray to God that way? If you ever did, I do not think you will do it a second time. I tried it once, but I am not likely to repeat the experiment. I thought I would try to pray to God in that fashion, but it did not seem to come naturally from me; and when I had done so, I thought I heard somebody at a distance saying, "God be merciful to me a sinner," and he went home to his house justified; and then I had to tear off my Pharisaic robes, and get back to where the poor publican had been standing, for his place and his prayer suited me admirably. I cannot make out what has happened to some of my brethren, who fancy themselves so wonderfully good. I wish the Lord would strip them of their self-righteousness, and let them see themselves as they really are in his sight. Their fine notions concerning the higher life would soon vanish then. Brethren, the highest life I ever hope to reach to, this side of heaven, is to say from my very soul—

"I the chief of sinners am,
But Jesus died for me."

I have not the slightest desire to suppose that I have advanced in the spiritual life many stages beyond my brethren. As long as I trust simply to the blood and righteousness of Christ, and think nothing of myself, I believe that I shall continue to be pleasing to the Lord Jesus Christ, that this joy will be in me, and that my joy will be full.

C. H. Spurgeon

Thus, although all Paul insists on here is that he does not belong to Christ any less than do his opponents, his protestation emerges from the matrix of a profound grasp of every Christian's indebtedness to grace, and from his utter revulsion of "Christian" one-upmanship.

Second, Paul points out that whatever authority has been entrusted to him, it was given for building believers up, not tearing them down. Indeed, the Greek text emphasizes the point by offering a suggestive comparison. Paul says, in effect, "I have boasted (in a rather paradoxical way) about belonging to Christ; but even if I boast about something beyond that, namely, the authority the Lord gave me [NIV's "even if I boast somewhat freely"], I will not be ashamed of it—that is, my boast would be substantiated by the facts. For the authority the Lord gave me was for the purpose of building up believers; and everyone knows I founded the church in Corinth and built you up. Can the self-proclaimed apostles, the intruders, claim so much? Have they not rather introduced friction and worldly categories that have pulled you down?"

Elsewhere (Gal 1:1,11-12,15-16), Paul emphasizes that both his call to apostolic ministry and the gospel he preaches are of divine origin. The ultimate source of his authority as an apostle, and the ultimate authority behind the gospel he proclaims, is God himself. In 2 Corinthians Paul occasionally stresses something similar (cf. 3:5-6; 13:10); but in this passage (10:8) his point is a little different: he emphasizes not so much the *origin* as the *purpose* of the authority about which he prefers not to boast. That purpose is beneficent—i.e., he wields his authority not to gain advantage for himself, or to promote himself, still less to tear others down, but to build up the church. This building-up language is an extension of the common metaphor of the church seen as a building or a temple, built on the foundation, Jesus Christ. Expert builder that he is, Paul builds on this foundation, and exhorts others to be careful what materials they use when it is their turn to build (1 Cor 3:10-17). Using the same metaphor, Paul says he was given authority to build up the Corinthians, not to pull them down, like a wrecker intent on demolishing a building.

Paul does not mean, of course, that he has no authority to exercise discipline or to pass judgment; for elsewhere he insists that if he is forced to take such unpleasant steps, he is not only prepared to do so but fully able to uphold his judgments (cf. 2 Cor. 13:1-4). He is not restricting himself to a polite power-of-positive-thinking approach, committed above all to offending no one, not even the devil himself. Rather, he is insisting that the central purpose of the authority entrusted to him is the edification (the building up) of God's people. In exactly the same way, the central purpose of the Son of God's coming into the world was *not* to condemn the world but to save the world (John 3:17)—even though one of the entailments of that coming is to pronounce judgment and doom on those who will not repent and believe. So Paul: he may have to wield the rod of discipline, but that is auxiliary to the central purpose of his mission and of the authority he exercises.

To the Corinthian believers, therefore, Paul is launching a challenge. They have heard the intruders putting Paul down on a number of points, not least in condescending dismissal of his authority. He responds that he prefers not to talk about the authority the Lord gave him (though if he did boast about it, he would not be ashamed—i.e., his claims would be valid); but he insists at the same time that whatever authority he has received, its purpose is to build up, not pull down—and thus he sidesteps the question of the origin of his authority and focuses the Corinthians' attention on the purpose and results of his authority. If they reflect only a little they would remember that Paul did the initial evangelization among them, founded their church, built them up in their faith, safeguarded them from various errors. The false apostles can claim none of those things. They have used their authority to criticize, divide a church, and lead God's people away from the gospel they intially clung to for salvation. Small wonder Paul tells them to look at the obvious facts (2 Cor. 10:7)! Their challenge is to free themselves from the false criteria being taught by the intruders, and to look again at indisputable evidence in Paul's favor.

It is true, of course, that results and effects do not always serve as adequate criteria of a valid ministry. Some faithful missionaries, e.g., have worked in particularly difficult areas and seen very little fruit; and conversely, some highly "successful" ministries may rightly be adjudged cultic. Gamaliel's advice (Acts 5:33-39)—that the trappings of success prove a movement is from God—is frequently false. Neverthe-less, the fruit of a person's ministry must be at least one of the factors to be borne in mind when that person claims the prerogatives of leadership. Paul subtly reminds the Corinthians that they are Christians because of his ministry, and implicitly asks, "What comparable purposes and results can the ministry of the interlopers claim?" Thus although fine purpose and results do not automatically guarantee valid ministry, they can provide some support for claims to divine authorization.

The principle is a profound one with many applications. How many Christians with meager service records spend large blocks of time criticizing more productive servants of God? In specific cases, it is of course possible that the criticism is just and the productive minister some brand of phony; but in most cases the critics are more like the intruding false apostles than they might care to admit. Paul's point is a challenge for Christian leaders in every generation: whatever authority is entrusted to them is for the purpose of building up fellow believers, not tearing them down.

The precise syntactical and logical connection between 2 Corinthians 10:8 and verse 9 is much disputed. It is possible there is an ellipsis (a few words left out, yet understood by both writer and reader). If so, the thought flows something like this: If I were to boast about the authority the Lord has given me—given me for building people up, not pulling them down—I would not be ashamed; *but I will not do so,* lest I seem to be frightening you with my letters." In other words, verse 9 provides additional reason why Paul will not boast of his God-given authority; for if he does so in this letter, his opponents will respond by saying his strong self-defense is typical of his weighty and forceful letters (v. 10), and completely atypical of his person. So Paul cleverly avoids the trap, and says, on the one hand, that if he chose to boast about his authority, there would in fact be substance to his claims; and on the other hand, that in any case this authority about which he chooses not to boast is for purposes of edification. The trap is wisely avoided; the important points are made.

Third, Paul insists he is consistent, contrary appearances notwithstanding. His opponents charged him with a literary false front: his letters might be weighty and forceful, but the real Paul, Paul in person, was (they said) unimpressive, and his speaking worthy of contempt. Paul responds by saying in effect that if the intruders continue making their accusations, they will bring down such wrath on their heads when Paul finally arrives that all will see the apostle is perfectly capable of taking them on in person and not through letters only: "Such people should realize that what we are in our letters when we are absent, we will be in our actions when we are present" (2 Cor 10:11).

How competent a speaker Paul was we cannot know. By the time of the first missionary journey he has emerged as the "chief speaker" (Acts 14:12) when he and Barnabas are on the road together; and the pagans of Lystra, mistaking them for gods because of a miracle they performed in Jesus' name, dub Paul "Hermes," the god who in Greek mythology carried messages; yet interestingly enough these citizens of Lystra did not mistake Paul for the brilliant, sonorous Apollos; and elsewhere Acts records that Paul's preaching could not keep Eutychus awake (Acts 20:9; cf. Plummer). What Paul certainly lacked were the rhetorical flourishes frankly expected of speakers in certain strands of Hellenistic society; but the charge leveled against him by the intruders transcends this perceived deficiency and charges Paul with a duplicitous inconsistency. That is why Paul responds by defending his consistency.

An old adage tells us, "Consistency is the hobgoblin of little minds." That is surely not quite right: some inconsistencies— moral, intellectual, logical, spiritual—cannot possibly be the characteristics of great minds. Yet the old adage has a point. It pithily reminds us that although great minds may presume profound consistency at the level of principle, they may be extraordinarily flexible at the level of practice—so flexible, in fact, that lesser minds may unjustly charge them with inconsistency, because lesser minds are frequently slow to discern the principles marked by the more obvious practices.

The apostle Paul was certainly one of the most flexible believers to emerge from the early church. Who but he could readily become a Jew to the Jews and a Gentile to the Gentiles, a slave to everyone so that by all possible means he might save some (1 Cor 9:19-23)? A fine example of his flexibility comes from his handling of circumcision. On the one hand, when certain Jews insisted that Gentiles had to come under the Mosaic covenant by being circumcised and become Jewish proselytes before they could legitimately come under the lordship of the Jewish Messiah Jesus, Paul strenuously objected. He perceived that the result of such advocacy was to deny the sufficiency of Jesus' cross-work and resurrection to restore men and women to God. And so Titus was not circumcised; for as Paul puts it, "We did not give in to them for a moment, so that the truth of the gospel might remain with you" (Gal 2:1-5). On the other hand, according to Luke, Paul was perfectly happy to circumcise Timothy (Acts 16:1-3); for in that situation no one was suggesting that Timothy had to be circumcised if he was to be saved. Rather, everyone knew that although his mother was a Jewess, his father was a Greek, and the young man had never been "done." This would have limited his usefulness as an assistant to Paul whenever the apostle attempted to enter synagogues and other Jewish centers to evangelize his own people.

Of course, a critic might charge Paul with inconsistency: the same Paul circumcises Timothy yet refuses to permit Titus to be circumcised. But those who knew Paul best, who understood the profound principles that dominated his life and thought, would have grasped the deep consistency implicit in these decisions. He was the sort of man who had such a profound grasp of the supremacy of the gospel, such a yearning to win people to Jesus Christ, and such balanced insight into the relationships between the old covenant and the new, that he felt perfectly comfortable eating meat the Old Testament forbade; yet he would not under any circumstances do so if he felt weaker brothers and sisters in Christ might have their faith harmed by his indulgence. He would gladly circumcise Christian males if it would increase the effectiveness of their witness, but would adamantly refuse to do so if it would jeopardize the sufficiency and exclusiveness of the gospel he loved and by which he was saved.

In a similar way, superficial observers, critics to a man, might charge Paul with inconsistency because they find his letters weighty and forceful but his personal presence unimpressive. But perhaps they have not considered certain relevant factors. Paul's forceful letters have been written in response to dire developments in the Corinthian church. If similar developments take place just before his personal visit, they will discover he can be no less forceful and severe in person (2 Cor 10:11; 13:2,10) than in his letters. And meanwhile the critics should not check their own criteria of contemporary rhetoric lest they be seduced by form and remain unresponsive to content and truth (cf. 11:6)?

Paul maintains he is consistent; and the intruders cannot fail to hear a veiled threat. For if Paul is right, then one day he will prove his point by displaying in person the forcefulness they deny he has; but then it will be directed toward their discipline and destruction.

B. Countercharge: Improper Boasting (10:12-18)

Throughout the embarrassed self-defense that characterizes so much of 2 Corinthians 10-13, it is easy to detect the range of charges and accusations levelled against Paul by the intruders. But here and there, Paul's firm statements enable us to detect what charges he is making against them in return. Nowhere is this clearer than in 10:12-18, where Paul's denials (vv. 12a, 13,14,15,18) betray his understanding of what the false apostles have been up to, what he charges against them. Indeed, at one point (v. 12b) he refers to them directly and presents a specific condemnation of their activity. The heart of Paul's countercharge in these verses is that their boasting is improper, their self-commendation unrestrained and dishonest, and their focus on man and not God. The text makes five crucial points:

1. Paul refuses to permit commendations to be definitive (10:12a). In this area Paul is indeed timid; he does not *dare* to classify or compare himself with some who commend themselves. Irony saturates Paul's "admission." Apparently Paul's opponents were given to writing flowery letters of recommendation for one another, and perhaps as well letters of self-introduction stacked with self-praise—the ancient equivalent of a modern, unrestrained *curriculum vitae.* But Paul has little time for self-commendation. Because he is so concerned to win the Lord's approval (l Cor 4:1-5), he does "not dare to classify or compare himself with some who commend themselves" (2 Cor 10:12).

Nevertheless, Paul is caught in a difficult situation. As Goudge comments, "Self-defence is almost impossible without self-commendation. S. Paul's opponents at Corinth made the former necessary, and then blamed him for the latter." Already in 2 Corinthians 3:1, after explaining a little how he preaches the gospel as a faithful servant of Christ, he has to ask, "Are we beginning to commend ourselves again? Or do we need, like some people, letters of recommendation to you or from you?" Surely not. Paul never was an apostle of men, sent out by them (Gal 1:1), but an apostle of Christ Jesus: and Christ's approval is all he seeks. He is of course glad to be commended by his own churches, since their coming into existence depended on him; but in that case their approval is nothing more than the courtesy of gratitude and a sign of their fidelity to the apostolic gospel. Their commendation of Paul is an acknowledgment, after the fact, of their dependence upon him, not a hurdle erected by them over which Paul must successfully leap if he is to secure their approval. As Paul tells the Corinthians, "You yourselves are our letter, written on our hearts, known and read by everybody. You show that you are a letter from Christ, the result of our ministry, written not with ink but with the Spirit of the living God, not on tablets of stones but on tablets of human hearts" (2 Cor 3:3-4).

In other words, far from needing letters from some unnamed source of authority in order for the Corinthians to accept his credentials, Paul claims the Corinthians themselves constitute his credentials, "written" by Christ in that Christ saved them and established them through Paul's ministry. If Paul is forced again and again to defend himself, it is not at all because he cares for the praise of men. Rather, as he explains to the Corinthians in another passage, "We are not trying to commend ourselves to you again, but are giving you an opportunity to take pride in us, so that you can answer those who take pride in what is seen rather than what is in the heart" (2 Cor 5:12). As he testifies elsewhere, "Even though I may not be an apostle to others, surely I am to you! For you are the seal of my apostleship in the Lord" (1 Cor 9:2).

Unfortunately, the Corinthians were so seduced by the

credential-waving false apostles that Paul is forced to use even stronger language and admit (with grim irony) that he would not "dare" use their procedures of extravangant self-glorification. He refuses to permit commendations to be definitive.

2. Paul insists that the lack of an objective standard is folly (10:12b). Paul is certainly not suggesting that there is no place at all for assessing competing claims. What he objects to so strongly about the intruders' procedures for self-enhancement is that they utilize no objective standard. They simply "measure themselves by themselves and compare themselves with themselves"; and in this, "they are not wise." Apparently these self-promoted apostles compared notes on their visions, their racial and cultural pedigrees, their training in rhetoric, their abilities to command fees and lead men—all relative criteria of little importance in God's eyes.

Doubtless these false apostles had no intention of measuring themselves by the objective criteria preferred by Paul— allegiance to the gospel of Christ, growing conformity to the character of Christ, participation in the sufferings of Christ. But they failed to see that self-assessment based on relative standards means no real self-assessment at all. It is impossible to gauge the speed of a moving train while standing in another moving train on an adjacent track (unless of course you know the speed and direction of your own train—but in that case your real standard of comparison is objective and external to both trains). It is no less impossible to gain very meaningful appraisal of moral rectitude or spiritual leadership by comparing leaders. Some absolute standard of reference is necessary. Worse, because the false apostles who had invaded the Corinthian church had a distorted understanding of themselves (as judged by the objective gospel Paul preached), they suffered equally from a profound inability to understand their environment and circumstances. There is no evidence that they could really see the damage they were inflicting on the church, the schisms they were introducing, the duplicity and hypocrisy intrinsic to their treatment of Paul.

The lack of an objective standard is folly. Of the many applications of this principle, we may consider two. The *first* is most like the situation in Corinth. Many modern Christians have become so enamoured of the styles of leadership found in politics or the entertainment industry that they are unwittingly transferring these essentially secular criteria to the church. Such secular criteria, however, are largely culturally conditioned, and swing with public opinion. The question Christians ought to ask about their aspiring leaders is: To what extent do they conform to biblical stipulations for the posts and functions they are considering? Repeated reading of, say, the pastoral epistles might help to change our thinking and bring it more closely into line with God's thinking. Those of us who are leaders might resort less often to name-dropping and politics, and become more concerned about prayer, winsome integrity, humility, and conformity to Jesus Christ.

A *second* and no less disturbing development is taking place in the mainstream of Western society. Western democracies were not founded exclusively by Christians (in the biblical sense); but by and large they were founded by disparate groups (including Deists, unconverted church people, and many others) the majority of whom adhered to the existence of a law higher than those passed by our legislatures. That higher law was broadly identified with the ideal moral standards of the Judaeo-Christian heritage. In the last few decades, however, this loose consensus has increasingly broken down. Rising numbers of people want freedom from such law. The deep tragedy is that as a result we argue for or against a piece of legislation on the sole grounds of expediency. The moral significance of legislation is not considered; or worse, the word "moral" is tossed around in a partisan way to justify any party's convictions without recourse to the constraints of a revealed higher law to which we are all accountable. The result is not greater liberty, but (from a biblical perspective) less virtue. Where there is less virtue, there will be more vice; and more vice inevitably leads to the destruction of society and the loss of freedom.

It is always true that the lack of an objective standard is folly. If we as Christians are to stand against the tide of modern relativism, whether in our churches or in the broader society, we shall have to fill our minds with the Word of God, well digested and integrated, and learn to think our way from God's thoughts to our situation with prayerful humility and a profound desire to assess all things, ourselves included, by criteria less arbitrary and relative than the shifting standards of the surrounding culture.

3. Paul outlines the limitation on boasting established by one's personal sphere of work (10:13-15a). By contrast with those who have no objective standard (2 Cor 10:12), Paul will "not boast beyond proper limits" (v. 13), i.e., without the limits of an objective standard, in an unmeasured way. For Paul, the measure or standard to be adopted (as he tells us elsewhere) is Christ Jesus himself (cf. 11:1; 4:10; 10:1); but the notion of measurement against an objective standard apparently calls to his mind an extension of this language to a slightly different "standard" or "field" (v. 13 NIV; "territory" in v. 16). Paul will confine his boasting, he says, to the field God has assigned him— i.e., to the geographical limitations of his own apostolic outreach—a field which (he wryly adds) reaches even to Corinth.

Some scholars have thought that Paul is referring primarily to the concordat of Galatians 2:9. Peter and the others agreed that they should evangelize primarily among the Jews, and recognized the grace given to Paul to go to the Gentiles. In the wake of Paul's conversion, God himself had declared, "This man is my chosen instrument to carry my name before the Gentiles" (Acts 9:15). What Paul is offended at, therefore, is the invasion of his essentially Gentile outreach by Judaizing intruders. Stated so boldly, this interpretation of these verses is too simple. Paul is glad for the help of others (e.g., Apollos, 1 Cor 3:5-10); and he was never the sort of person to put down those who were preaching the same gospel as he, even if their motives could not always stand close scrutiny (e.g., Phil 1:15-18). Yet there is some validity to the interpretation; for it is hard to imagine that, whether or not they came from Jerusalem, the intruding rivals had no knowledge at all of the agreement between Paul and the other apostles. If they knew that the Jerusalem apostles had agreed that Paul should exercise his apostolic ministry primarily among the Gentiles, it was vile of them to spend their energies demeaning his ministry, especially among his own Gentile converts.

The explicit thrust of this passage, however, is less racial than geographical. Paul's apostolic ministry had extended to Corinth; and by this means the Corinthians themselves had come to know the Savior. Ironically, by questioning Paul's legitimacy the Corinthians are almost questioning the legitimacy of their own conversion!

Paul sees the "field" or "territory" in which he has done the primary evangelism and church planting as the "measure" God has given him, not only because of his commission to preach to Gentiles, and not only because of his sense of God's leading in the geographical decisions and turnings he made, but also because in God's providence he got to Corinth first. The clause rendered "we did get as far as you" (2 Cor 10:14) includes a verb that can indeed mean "reach" or "attain" or "get as far as" (cf. also Rom 9:31; Phil 3:16); but a slightly fuller sense of the Greek verb is preserved in 1 Thessalonians 4:15, where it means "to precede," i.e., to go first or to reach first. That admirably suits the context in 2 Corinthians 10:14: "we were the first to reach you" (NEB). After all, the intruders had also reached Corinth: in that sense Paul was no different from any other preacher, false or true, who managed to make the trip to Corinth and exercise a little ministry. But Paul was the first to reach the Corinthians; and that was a claim that could never be successfully challenged or overturned. It was forever fixed, a claim no subsequent event could diminish, and a reflection of Paul's own profound sense of God's call to primary evangelism and church planting. Corinth was part of the "field" God had assigned Paul.

The thought is not far removed from the presentation Paul makes of his ministry to the Romans. "I glory in Christ Jesus in my service to God," he writes. "I will not venture to speak of anything except what Christ has accomplished through me in leading the Gentiles to obey God by what I have said and done—by the power of signs and miracles, through the power of the Spirit. So from Jerusalem all the way around to Illyricum, I have fully proclaimed the gospel of Christ. It has always been my ambition to preach the gospel where Christ was not known, so that I would not be building on someone else's foundation" (15:17-20).

By contrast, the intruders were not so scrupulous. They made it a practice to boast of work done by others (2 Cor

10:15). We have already discovered that Paul has no objection to people who build on the foundation he lays (1 Cor 3:10); but these intruding apostles appear to have gone well beyond that point. They probably boasted that whatever spiritual vitality the Corinthians displayed was due to their ministry—even though they were latecomers to the scene and occupied themselves by diminishing the authority of the founding apostle. Small wonder they pursued this occupation, of course, if they were trying to introduce new doctrine incompatible with what Paul taught (2 Cor 11:4); but it was pretty disgusting conduct just the same.

These petty little men could not approach the high standards that characterized Paul's ministry; yet somehow they gave themselves such airs that they managed to seduce much of the Corinthian church. Little men can be dangerous, especially when they position themselves in such a way as to capture some stolen glory from great men, and forge it into the bangles of self-interested leadership.

The boasting of the false apostles at Corinth was deeply improper. Not only was it steeped in self-commendation and without objective standards, it was hypocritically parasitical on the work of the very apostle they were demeaning. As if that were not enough, Paul adds two further elements to his countercharge and exposes the impropriety of their boasting at deep levels.

4. Paul lays out certain constraints of vision on boasting (10:15b-16). "Our hope is that, as your faith continues to grow, our area of activity among you will greatly expand, so that we can preach the gospel in the regions beyond you." The hope of the intruders is to steal Paul's sheep. Paul's hope is so to consolidate his ministry among the Corinthians that he will be free to press on to fresh, unevangelized regions. Paul reiterates that he does "not want to boast about work already done in another man's territory" (2 Cor 10:16b); but this is not simply a repetition of his rebuke of the intruders, it is a testimony to his own vision, his own chomping at the bit in the light of the need and his own calling. Others are busy forging reputations for themselves on the basis of his work; Paul himself is already fastening his hope on the next stage of his work. The constraints of his ongoing concern and vision limit both his desire and his ability to boast. The little men busily brag about one church to which they have little claim; the apostle himself sees the enormity of the task, feels the call of God on his life, and has no time for or interest in boasting. His desire rather is to stabilize the faith of the Corinthian believers so that he may leave them behind and press on to new territory and new challenges.

There are four lessons to be learned. *First*, boasting is irretrievably bound up with the past, whereas the truly fruitful servants of God keep looking to the future. Paul has his mind on Rome (Acts 19:21b; Rom 1:11) and beyond Rome on Spain and the western Mediterranean (15:24,28). The false apostles have their eyes on taking over what Paul has already done. *Second*, real expansion of the church comes, not by poaching or by moving van evangelism, but by proclaiming the gospel in areas and among people where the Lord Jesus Christ is not known. *Third*, the fact that Paul wants to consolidate the gains in Corinth before moving on testifies to the importance of full-orbed discipleship, of building churches and not just winning converts. In a sense, Paul is prepared to mortgage his own vision of the future to the needs of the Corinthian church. If God called him to establish a church in Corinth, he cannot abandon that responsibility just because he detects new opportunities and still greater needs elsewhere. Consolidation is the foundation on which to launch new advance. "How could he prosecute pioneer evangelism in the western Mediterranean when his converts in the western Mediterranean were unsettled and in danger of apostasy (11:3)?" (Harris). *Fourth*, although many of us may be called by God simply to carry the torch of truth from one generation to another (cf. 2 Tim 2:2), it is encouraging to learn of believers like Caleb who size up the difficulties and choose in God's strength to tackle the toughest assignments (Josh 14:10-12). Not every apostle set his heart on Spain or India; but we may thank God for those who did, and lovingly, prayerfully support the new generation of ambassadors who hunt out the most difficult tasks—Muslim evengelism, working among the most forsaken, the poorest, the most diseased, the most hardened. And some of us, at least, should ask ourselves whether God might not want us to abandon our padded pulpits and expand the horizons of our ministry by planting new churches in hard places.

Even familiarity with such breadth of vision will provide needed restraints on our boasting.

5. Finally, Paul overthrows all self-interested boasting (10:17,18). He accomplishes this by quoting a line from the prophet Jeremiah, one he had earlier used in writing to the Corinthians (1 Cor 1:31). Probably therefore they were familiar with the surrounding lines from that prophet.

> This is what the LORD says:
> "Let not the wise man boast of his wisdom
>   or the strong man boast of his strength
>   or the rich man boast of his riches,
> but let him who boasts boast about this:
>   that he understands and knows me,
>   that I am the LORD who exercises kindness,
>   justice and righteousness on earth,
>   for in these things I delight,"
>   declares the LORD.
>
>   (Jer 9:23-24)

The intruding false apostles thought they were wise and strong; and probably their fee structures made them wealthy as well. But the Lord (almost certainly a reference to the Lord Jesus) forbids all such boasting. Only one kind of boasting does he permit—indeed, command: and that is boasting in the Lord. Paul is prepared to boast what God has done for him (Gal 6:14) in the cross of the Lord Jesus Christ, and what God has done through him (Rom 15:18-19; cf. Acts 14:27) by the Spirit in his apostolic ministry; but he is not prepared to boast about talent, wealth, power, wisdom, eloquence, and the like. After all, what do we have but what we have received (1 Cor 4:7)? If we forget this we succumb to a form of idolatry; if we remember in what proper boasting consists, we boast in the Lord—which means that we give him the praise rightly his due. He is the God who declares, "I will not yield my glory to another" (Isa 48:11; cf. 42:8).

Paul understands that what ultimately matters is whether or not we gain the Lord's approval. The verses cited from Jeremiah are followed by the Lord's promise of judgment (9:25). Paul brings us up short the same way: what matters most in God's universe is what God thinks of us, whether we are approved by him (2 Cor 10:18). The person who commends himself is certainly not impressing the Lord; presumably he must be trying to impress other people and win their approval. But the man who is approved by the Lord must be the one whom the Lord commends. Will he commend those who boast in precisely the way he forbids? Will he not rather commend those who boast in him—who rely on his grace and acknowledge his power, forgiveness, gifts, and sovereign sway, and delight to make them known?

The crux of the division between Paul and his opponents is the question, "Whose approval do we seek?" That brief question, properly considered against the background of the revelation of truth in the Scriptures and in Jesus Christ, cuts through many moral dilemmas and orients us to pleasing God. Paul's desire was to please the Lord Christ throughout his life and service, and then at the final tribunal to hear Christ's "Well done!" This is the final constraint Paul puts on boasting, and any boasting that fails this test must be rejected as improper. Not only nations, but the church herself, needs to pray,

> God of our fathers, known of old . . .
> The tumult and the shouting dies;
> The captains and the kings depart:
> Still stands thine ancient sacrifice,
> An humble and a contrite heart.
> Lord God of hosts, be with us yet,
> Lest we forget—lest we forget! . . .
>
> For heathen heart that puts her trust
> In reeking tube and iron shard,
> All valiant dust that builds on dust,
> And, guarding, calls not Thee to guard,
> For frantic boast and foolish word—
> Thy mercy on Thy People, Lord!

> Rudyard Kipling (1865-1936)

The Danger
of False Apostleship
Overturning False Criteria

2 Corinthians 11:1-15

¹ I hope you will put up with a little of my foolishness: but you are already doing that. ² I am jealous for you with a godly jealousy. I promised you to one husband, to Christ, numbers are so that I might present you as a pure virgin to him. ³ But I am afraid that just as Eve was deceived by the serpent's cunning, your minds may somehow be led astray from your sincere and pure devotion to Christ. ⁴ For if someone comes to you and preaches a Jesus other than the Jesus we preached, or if you receive a different spirit from the one you received, or a different gospel from the one you accepted, you put up with it easily enough. ⁵ But I do not think I am in the least inferior to those "super-apostles." ⁶ I may not be a trained speaker, but I do have knowledge. We have made this perfectly clear to you in every way.

⁷ Was it a sin for me to lower myself in order to elevate you by preaching the gospel of God to you free of charge? ⁸ I robbed other churches by receiving support from them so as to serve you. ⁹ And when I was with you and needed something, I was not a burden to anyone, for the brothers who came from Macedonia supplied what I needed. I

have kept myself from being a burden to you in any way, and will continue to do so. [10] As surely as the truth of Christ is in me, nobody in the regions of Achaia will stop this boasting of mine. [11] Why? Because I do not love you? God knows I do! [12] And I will keep on doing what I am doing in order to cut the ground from under those who want an opportunity to be considered equal with us in the things they boast about.

[13] For such men are false apostles, deceitful workmen, masquerading as apostles of Christ. [14] And no wonder, for Satan himself masquerades as an angel of light. [15] It is not surprising, then, if his servants masquerade as servants of righteousness. Their end will be what their actions deserve.

P aul is still sidling up to the boasts he must make in order to prevent the Corinthian believers from being further seduced by the false apostles. His boasts are concentrated in 2 Corinthians 11:16-12:10; but here in 11:1-15 he is still preparing the ground. This preparation involves three steps. First, he exhorts his readers to put up with his "foolishness" as he shifts ground and contemplates the ugly prospect of putting his claims alongside those of the intruders (vv. 1-6). Then he handles one more specific charge (vv. 7-12) before exposing the troublemakers for what they are (vv. 13-15). Only after he has presented his own perspectives so clearly is Paul prepared, at last, to stoop to the level of his opponents for the sake of maintaining the faith of his converts.

A. Exhortation to Put Up with Paul's Foolishness (11:1-6)

In the last chapter we discovered that the word "boasting" crops up regularly in this part of 2 Corinthians. Now another word-group joins it: "foolishness" or "fool" or "foolish" (11:1,16,17,19,21; 12:6,11). Boasting is utterly repugnant to Paul. "As much against the grain as it is with a proud man to acknowledge his infirmities, so much is it against the grain with a humble man to speak in his own praise" (Henry). He has repeatedly insisted to the Corinthians that self-commendation is worthless (3:1; 5:12; 10:12); but the situation before him appears to demand that he stoop to what he condemns if he is going to preserve his converts. He is forced in part to ape his opponents' methods, even if he distances himself entirely from their motives. As Tasker puts it:

> Paul is very conscious that it is no business of an apostle, or indeed of any Christian, to praise himself. Such self-commendation is only justified, in the present instance, because his affection for his converts is so great, that he will go to almost any length to prevent them from becoming dupes of unscrupulous men, and to keep them loyal to Christ.

This extreme to which Paul is prepared to go is what he calls his "foolishness"; and later on, when he actually begins to boast, he insists he is not talking as a Christian would, but as a "fool" (11:17). This is not exactly the same use of "fool" as in 1 Corinthians 4:10, where Paul says, "We apostles are fools for Christ." In that passage, he means that he and the other apostles are regarded as fools by the world. But here in 2 Corinthians 10-13, he is prepared to be "foolish" in the sense that he is willing for the sake of his converts to engage for a few moments in conduct he regards as fundamentally distasteful, sub-Christian, foolish.

"I hope you will put up with a little of my foolishness," Paul writes, intensely embarrassed by the prospect of his imminent boasting; and then he adds, with delicious irony, "but you are already doing that" (2 Cor 11:1). What he means is that in one sense the Corinthians, misled by the intruders, have begun to treat him as if he were a second class clown, a fool, rather than their father through the gospel (1 Cor 4:15) and the apostle to the Gentiles. If the Corinthians can put up with his foolishness as *they* measure foolishness, surely they will put up with a little of his foolishness as *he* measures foolishness! Alternatively, it is just possible he means something a little different, but no less ironical: the Corinthians have already shown they are prepared to put up with the species of conduct Paul calls foolishness, for it is just such conduct that characterizes the intruders. Paul hopes they can put up with a little of his foolishness; but after all, it shouldn't be too difficult, he suggests, since the believers in Corinth have had a lot of practice in putting up with exactly the same foolishness in others.

The next five verses provide three reasons why Paul expects the Corinthians to put up with the foolish boasting in which he is about to engage:[1]

1. Because Paul is divinely jealous for the Corinthians (11:2-3). "I am jealous for you," Paul writes, "with a godly jealousy." Some might hastily (and wrongly) respond that there can never be anything godly about jealousy: "godly jealousy" must be a contradiction in terms. But such an opinion forgets that God himself declares, "You shall not make for yourself an idol. . . . You shall not bow down to them or worship them; for I, the LORD your God, am a jealous God" (Exod 20:4,5). The same attitude can be expressed in other terms:

> "What can I do with you, Ephraim?
> What can I do with you, Judah?
> Your love is like the morning mist,
> like the early dew that disappears"

> (Hos 6:4).

Most human jealousy is a vice. It seeks to diminish or consume its object, and it is motivated by resentment, envy, and self-interest. Even the few types of legitimate human jealousy (as when a wife, say, is jealous of her husband as she is forced to reflect on his promiscuous behavior) are often contaminated by sinful strains. Very little human jealousy is really pure.

Divine jealousy, by contrast, is a virtue. It is a form of holy outrage mingled with love: the objects of the jealousy owe their love and allegiance to God, solemnly pledge him their filial devotion and covenantal obedience, receive all they have of strength and health and possessions and reason from his gracious hand—and then proudly strut their self-proclaimed independence before his face. Worse, they sell themselves to false lords, masters who take everything and give nothing. God is rightly outraged: he would be less than holy were this not his response. Yet at the same time he loves his wayward people, and grieves over their self-inflicted prostitution and hurt. That he is a jealous God reflects the marvellous fact that he cannot be

---

1. The three reasons are structurally clearer in Greek than in English: each one is introduced by a *gar*.

reduced to the impassable Unmoved Mover of Aristotle and of many Deists. Sovereign and transcendent, he is also personal. When his holiness is affronted he is rightly wrathful, for the created order is his, and every sin is nothing less than rebellion against his rightful authority; when his covenant people prostitute themselves, he is rightly jealous, for they have not only broken solemn oaths and sullied their allegiance but they have spurned the God who bought them.

Paul claims to share something of this godly jealousy, this mixture of love, outrage, and fear: love for the Corinthians manifest in deep concern for their spiritual well-being; outrage at their fickleness, the ease and speed by which they have been seduced; fear for their future if they do not repent and return to the Lord.

Paul fleshes out his jealousy in a more extended metaphor. The metaphor is based in an Old Testament picture: Israel is the bride, and God is the bridegroom (e.g., Isa 50:1; 54:1-6; Ezek 16; Hos 1-3). This picture is slightly altered in the New Testament: the church is the bride, and the Lord Jesus is the heavenly bridegroom (e.g., Eph 5:22-23; Rev 19:7; 21:2,9; 22:17). Paul extends this picture one step further. He presents himself as the father of the bride, thus bringing together in one composite metaphor the image of himself as a spiritual father of the church (1 Cor 4:15; 2 Cor 12:14), and the common image of the church as a bride. In this fuller picture, the betrothal took place when Paul led the Corinthians to Christ and founded the church: "I promised you . . . to Christ, so that I might present you as a pure virgin to him" (11:2b). Betrothals in the ancient world were binding: there were no casual engagements, and a sexual fling by a betrothed woman would be viewed as nothing less than adultery. Paul, acting as the father, has betrothed the Corinthian church to Christ. As an honorable father, he desires to present his daughter as a pure virgin to her prospective husband when he comes for her (at the parousia). Instead, Paul hears reports that she is playing around with other lovers, and he is appalled. More, he is jealous for his daughter (not "of" her, but "for" her): incensed at the seducers, lovingly concerned for her purity and her future, hurt, outraged at her fickleness.

Paul makes a further comparison: "I am afraid that just as Eve was deceived by the serpent's cunning, your minds may

somehow be led astray from your sincere and pure devotion to
Christ" (2 Cor 11:3). Much intertestamental Jewish literature
interprets the deception of Eve (Gen 3) as a sexual seduction;
but Paul does not go so far. As he spins out the comparison,
the apostle draws a parallel in the deception involved in the two
cases, and expresses concern for the Corinthians' *mind.* They
once manifested "sincere and pure devotion to Christ"; but now
they are in danger of being deceived—like Eve. When Eve fell,
it was not because she was battered into sinful submission to
a wicked overlord, but because she was taken in by cunning.
She was not sufficiently devoted to the God who made her and
whose will sustained her in creaturely dependence, to withstand
the blandishments that enticed her away from proper allegiance
("Did God really say . . .?" Gen 3:1) and promised to give her
a new and exalted position ("and you will be like God," v. 3:5).
Tragically, the new position did not make Eve like God; it was, in
fact, characterized by death and corruption. How like the Corinthian situation! This betrothed community was not so devoted to
her husband that she could not be taken in by cunning. She is
being drawn away from her public allegiance, and is coyly
following the same old deceiver, Satan himself, as he leads her
into what seems to be a more triumphant, victorious, and self-
centered Christianity, but which is in reality no gospel at all
(2 Cor 11:4; 13:5).

Paul sees in these intruders, not casual competition, but the
machinations of the archfiend. The reason the Corinthians do
not recognize their own danger is because the enemy of their
spiritual welfare has used cunning. In fact, he is so cunning that
he has persuaded the Corinthians it is Paul who is "crafty" and
"tricky" (12:16; in Greek "crafty" is the same word as "cunning"
in 11:3)!

From the time of the Fall to the present day, men and women
have frequently succumbed to the deceptive devices of the devil.
Christians are especially open to the kind of cunning deceit that
combines the language of faith and religion with the content of
self-interest and flattery. We like to be told how special we are,
how wise, how blessed, especially if as a consequence others are
gently diminished. We like to have our Christianity shaped less
by the cross than by triumphalism or rules or charismatic
leaders or subjective experience. And if this shaping can be

coated with assurances of orthodoxy, complete with cliché, we may not detect the presence of the archdeceiver, nor see that we are being weaned away from "sincere and pure devotion to Christ" to a "different gospel." The danger of being deceived is so ubiquitous that Paul will shortly address it directly, and in the strongest terms (2 Cor 11:13-15).

Small wonder, then, that Paul is jealous for the Corinthians. But Paul's jealousy is a godly jealousy: it has the highest motives and an unselfish object. Most human jealousy is tinged with selfishness (indeed sometimes it is the very embodiment of the most concentrated self-interest), and often its object is unworthy. But Paul's jealousy reflects the heart of God, so much so that it is difficult to conceive of valid Christian leadership that does not in some measure manifest the same jealousy. How concerned is an elder, e.g., for the spiritual well-being of the believers he serves if he is not jealous for them with a godly jealousy? Christian ministry can never be merely professional. On the truth of the gospel hang eternal consequences. Therefore far from making aloof, analytical detachment the goal of Christian leaders, we will hunger for the clear-sighted and empathetic commitment of an apostle who can ask, "Who is weak, and I do not feel weak? Who is led into sin, and I do not inwardly burn?" (2 Cor 11:29).

What is scarcely less remarkable is the candor by which Paul advances his godly jealousy as a reason why the Corinthians should put up with his foolish boasting. The intensity of his love for them, the solemnity of the betrothal he has arranged between the Corinthian church and Christ, his fear that they will be deceived, should provide them with motive enough to put up with the "foolishness" on which he is about to embark.

But if Paul's godly jealousy is insufficient reason, he provides them with another. The Corinthians should gladly hear Paul out, foolishness and all:

2. Because they accept all kinds of nonsense from the rival apostles easily enough (11:4). "For if someone comes to you and preaches a Jesus other than the Jesus we preached, or if you receive a different spirit from the one you received, or a different gospel from the one you accepted, you put up with it easily enough." The introductory "for" probably serves a double function: it grounds the fear expressed and the appeal to put up with Paul. In other words, Paul is afraid that the Corinthians are being deceived (11:3), *for* they are much too tolerant of those who teach heresy (11:4); and Paul continues to appeal to the Corinthians to put up with his foolishness, *for* after all they gladly put up with a competing message that is fundamentally false. "Surely they should show their father in the faith the same degree of tolerance showed a newcomer preaching a different faith!" (Harris)

The exact shape of the false message the intruders preached is unclear. The best guess, judging from the emphases in the surrounding chapters, is that it was some form of Judaizing (see above, chap. 1). The false apostles made much of their Jewish heritage (2 Cor 11:22), and to this added a parade of virtues they felt made them superior Christians; or perhaps they even argued that some of these advantages were necessary requirements for true Christianity. Paul detected in their pretensions exactly the same danger that Judaizers with slightly different emphases introduced into the churches of Galatia. The result of their additions is that another Jesus is being preached (11:4; cf. Gal 1:8-9).

Of course in one sense they preached the same Jesus: they too doubtless believed he was the promised Messiah, that he performed miracles and preached the kingdom of God, that he died, rose from the grave, and ascended to the Father's right hand. Yet as soon as Jesus Christ is not the sole basis for our salvation, as soon as our acceptability before God depends on something more than his sacrifice on the cross, we have denied the *sufficiency* of his person and work. At that point the Jesus being preached is no longer the biblical Jesus, but an unreal product of human imagination, a relatively powerless figure who cannot effectively save his people from their sins unless they supplement his work with something of their own merit.

The sort of teaching to which the Corinthians were listening resulted as well in a different spirit. It is not entirely certain whether there is a reference to the Holy Spirit here; but probably not. The point rather is that the message of the true gospel, of sins forgiven, and the dawning of new and eternal life, brings a spirit of peace, freedom, power, love, and self-discipline (cf. Rom 14:17; 2 Cor 3:17; 2 Tim 1:7). But if believers revert to a legalistic system in which trust in Christ and joyous responsiveness to him are displaced by dependence upon personal merit and virtues, many will fall again into a spirit of slavery and fear that masks the privileges of our sonship (Rom 8:15). In sum, what is being preached is a different gospel.

When Paul criticizes the Corinthians for bowing to a Jesus "other than the Jesus we preached" or for accepting a gospel "different from the one you accepted," he is not claiming that the truth depends on him. He is far from saying, "Whatever I preach is right and true, just because I preach it. Just take my word for it and bow to my authority, and all will be well." It is not his own authority that captivates Paul, but the objective veracity of the gospel he preaches. That is why he can say elsewhere, "But *even if we* or an angel from heaven should preach a gospel other than the one we preached to you, let him be eternally condemned!" (Gal 1:8). Paul is so convinced of the truthfulness, the exclusive truthfulness, of the gospel he has been preaching, that if he himself were to change the shape of his preaching he can only wish damnation on himself. Here is no self-centered autocrat but a man who humbly sets himself under the revealed gospel and who is passionately committed to its proclamation and purity because he understands that alternative gospels are really no gospel (no "good news") at all. How different from the false apostles who in certain respects were apparently more interested in form and show than content (2 Cor 10:10; 11:6; cf. 1 Cor 1:17; 2:1,4-5), and whose self-centered triumphalism, frequently the handmaid of merit theology, produced a synthesis far removed from the biblical Jesus and the historic gospel.

The Christian church needs a little more both of Paul's discernment and intolerance. Like the ancient Corinthians, we too are sometimes deceived. Provided there is fluent talk of Jesus, gospel, truth, Christian living, and spiritual experience, combined with effective, self-confident leadership, we seldom ask if it is the same Jesus as the one presented in the Scriptures, or if the gospel being presented squares with the apostolic gospel. Most who read these pages will already have come to recognize that the Jesus preached by, say, the Jehovah's Witnesses is not in every respect like the Jesus of the New Testament. The total synthesis of the Witnesses results in another Jesus. But the same can be true of some presentations of Jesus that are closer to home. Is it a biblical Jesus who promises us nothing but health, prosperity, wisdom, and joy? Is it a biblical Jesus who guarantees heaven and says nothing of hell? Is it a biblical Jesus who promises eternal life but says nothing about entailed righteousness? Is it a biblical Jesus who needs to have his saving work supplemented by our merits, ceremonies, and sacrifices if we are to be redeemed? If the Corinthians could be deceived in the first century into transferring their allegiance to a Jesus who did not really exist, what entitles us to think we shall always be exempt from similar dangers and deceptions? Our only safeguard is a humble return, again and again, to the apostolic gospel, the biblical Jesus, preserved for us in the pages of Scripture.

The propensity of the Corinthians to follow a false gospel that is no gospel at all is the reason Paul is afraid that the Corinthians will be steered away from devotion to Christ; and it is also the reason Paul advances, in ironic tone, for giving him a hearing. He now adds one more:

3. Because Paul is not inferior to the "super-apostles" (11:5-6). These verses are again introduced, in Greek, by a "For." The Corinthians should put up with the foolish presentation Paul is about to make, *for*, he says, "I do not think I am in the least inferior to those 'super-apostles'."

Some scholars strongly argue that the super-apostles to whom Paul refers are not the intruders (whom he castigates as false apostles in 2 Cor 11:13-15), but apostles of genuine eminence— presumably the Twelve, held up as models, perhaps, by the interlopers. These scholars argue that Paul would not compare himself with these super-apostles if they were in fact the same people he labels deceitful workmen and servants of Satan a few verses later. This interpretation is plausible enough; but it overlooks the fact that Paul does in fact compare himself with the false apostles (e.g., vv. 22-23): that is the very heart of the foolish boasting to which he must resort. After all, Paul is not comparing himself with the false apostles in every way, but only on select fronts, in his attempt to regain the confidence of the Corinthians. And even when he draws such comparisons, two features stand out: first, he no sooner introduces a category in which comparisons are to be made, than he overturns the criteria of the intruders and adopts better ones (see esp. vv. 6,23-

28); and second, his pen drips irony throughout these chapters. "I do not think I am in the least inferior" is not a cold, calculating measurement, but sardonic irony designed to shame the Corinthians into reevaluation. Moreover, I have already shown (in chap. 1) that there are structural reasons for linking these super-apostles with the "false apostles" of verses 13-15.

It appears, then, that Paul offers, as a third reason why the Corinthians should put up with his "foolishness," his own conviction that he is not inferior to intruders who are demeaning him: and he alludes to their despicable conduct in this respect by calling his opponents, with deep irony, super-apostles. The specific point of comparison is the speaking ability of Paul and his opponents. Many sophisticated audiences in the Greek-speaking world favored a certain stylized rhetoric; and not to come up to rhetorical eloquence was considered a mark of inferior training or ability.

Paul concedes he is not a trained speaker (2 Cor 11:6). At first glance, therefore, Paul seems to be admitting that in this sense he is inferior after all. But this is too hasty a reading of the passage; for elsewhere Paul insists in no uncertain terms that he self-consciously rejected rhetorical flourishes in his own ministry, precisely so that his converts might find their faith resting on God's power and not on man's stylized wisdom (1 Cor 2:4-5). So also here: Paul appears to concede a point, but in reality he changes criteria. "I may not be a trained speaker," he says, "but I do have knowledge." And then, lest they fail to catch the point, he stresses it: "We have made this perfectly clear to you in every way" (2 Cor 11:6; that is probably the best rendering of some very difficult Greek).

It appears, then, from Paul's concern to maintain the true gospel and the real Jesus (2 Cor 11:4), and from his insistence that he has knowledge—i.e., knowledge of the true gospel—that the Corinthians were in danger of being seduced by a certain delectable form. Stylized rhetoric mattered more than truth. An infant might be more intrigued by the wrapping paper than the parcel it envelops; but no one else should be. Paul is not inferior as a preacher after all—provided the right criteria are used!

It may well be that even on formal grounds Paul was a better preacher than he here lets on. His concession is with respect to a certain artificial standard of oratory; but he may nevertheless have been a powerful and persuasive natural speaker who refused to adopt the unnatural standards of a particular rhetorical style. Such standards come and go; and while they are "in," they are dangerous insofar as they detract attention from content. Saying things in the approved, clever way may suddenly become more important than what you say.

This danger has often returned to haunt the church in one form or another. In the fourth century, John Chrysostom (c. 344-407) complained about his fellow Christian preachers who tried to emulate pagan oratory:

> There are many preachers who make long sermons: if they are well applauded, they are as glad as if they had obtained a kingdom; if they bring the sermon to an end in silence, their despondency is worse, I may almost say, than hell. It is this that wins churches, that you do not seek to hear sermons that touch the heart, but sermons that will delight your ears with intonation and the structure of their phrases, just as if you were listening to singers and lute-players. And we preachers humour your fancies, instead of trying to crush them.
>
> (Hom.30 on Act Apost.3)

In the last century, the great British preacher Charles Haddon Spurgeon lectured his students in these words:

> You may go all round, to church and chapel alike, and you will find that by far the larger majority of our preachers have a holy tone for Sundays. They have one voice for the parlour and the bedroom, and quite another tone for the pulpit; so that, if not double-tongued sinfully they certainly are so literally. The moment some men shut the pulpit door, they leave their own personal manhood behind them, and become as official as the parish beadle. There they might almost boast with the Pharisee, that they are not as other men are, although it would be blasphemy to thank God for it. No longer are they carnal and speak as men, but a whine, a broken hum-haw, an *ore rotundo*, or some other graceless mode of noise-making, is adopted, to prevent all suspicion of being natural and speaking out of the abundance of the heart. When that gown is once on, how often does it prove to be the shroud of the man's true self, and the effeminate emblem of officialism!
>
> (Lectures to My Students)

In many churches we do not face exactly the same problem today, the problem of profoundly artifical oratory. But we face other influences from our pagan surroundings, influences that have often so affected the form of our worship and ministry that attention has been drawn away from Christ. In many circles, congregations routinely applaud the special music (little of which is very special), and sometimes even the sermon. Thus we set up an atmosphere of interaction between performer and spectators, between entertainer and appreciative audience. This goes far beyond godly encouragement to those who serve well, and approaches the protocol of the theater. I have preached in enough of those circles to learn how to turn the applause on and off—and that of course is part of the insidious danger of it all, as Chrysostom understood. And gradually, congregations become more and more discerning in matters of form, and less and less discerning in matters of truth. We are developing new and powerful traditions that to some extent muzzle the gift of discernment, and expose us to essentially pagan ways of looking at corporate worship. A little thoughtful, self-critical reflection turns up countless numbers of such developments. Their total impact on the church, on truth, on pure devotion to Christ, on the quality of Christian leadership, cannot yet be fully estimated; but their essentially pagan character and deleterious contribution to self-interest as opposed to God's interest can scarcely be doubted.

Although Paul has used these verses to provide a third reason why the Corinthians should hear him out, foolishness and all— viz., because he is not inferior to the super-apostles—he has done so by challenging their fundamental criteria. There will be many more reversals of criteria before he is through (see esp. 2 Cor 11:21b-33; 12:1-10).

B. Answer to a Specific Charge:
Paul's Independence from the Corinthians (11:7-12)

Before embarking, at last, on his "foolish boasting" (2 Cor 11:16-12:10), Paul pinpoints one more specific area where his apostolicity has been called into question, and where the criteria used by his opponents are fundamentally evil.

Traveling teachers in the first century, professional sophists and rhetoricians, did not normally work with their hands. The best of them avoided begging, even if some manual work was required; but the ideal was to make a good living from teaching itself. The more famous the teacher, the more he could charge, and the more students would attach themselves to him and count it a privilege to pay his fee. Thus in many ways a teacher's status could be assessed by the price he could command, much as a figure on the modern college or political lecture circuit can be ranked by the size of his fee.

Unlike his sophist contemporaries, and unlike his intruding opponents, Paul has refused to accept any support at all from the Corinthian believers. It is not absolutely clear why he has taken this decision. Certainly Paul recognizes the principle that those who preach the gospel have the right of support from the people to whom they minister (see esp. 1 Cor 9; cf. 3 John 5-8), a principle that goes back to Jesus himself (Luke 9:3,4; 10:4,7). Moreover, Paul on occasion received financial help from the churches he founded: in particular, he received support from the churches of Macedonia, such as the church in Philippi (2 Cor 11:8-9; Phil 4:10-15), and he could also on occasion actively solicit assistance for his travels and ministry (Rom 15:24). True, Paul sometimes refused to take any money just so the gospel could be preached free of charge (1 Cor 9:16-18); but since that was not his universal practice, why does he refuse money from the Corinthians, especially when the issue has become such a sensitive one? Why not accept the money and thereby defuse the explosive situation? The Corinthians, after all, were aware that Paul had received help from other churches (and if they didn't know before 2 Corinthians was written, he candidly informs them of the fact in this letter, 11:8-9). Why should he treat them any differently?

Carefully tutored by the false apostles, already prejudiced by the surrounding pagan society to assess teachers by the size of their take, the Corinthians came to believe that Paul could not be much of an apostle after all. Perhaps they began to think of him the way Antiphon thought of Socrates:

> If you set any value on your own society, you would insist on getting the price for that too. It may well be that you are a just

man because you do not cheat people through avarice; but wise you cannot be since your knowledge is not worth anything.

Xenophon (*Memorabilia 1.6.12*)

Faced with such a deep bias, one that erects a condition of apostolicity, or at least a form of ranking, Paul attacks the problem head on. Once again he calls in question the evil criteria used by his opponents and naively adopted by the Corinthian church. He does this by presenting his own perceptions of the matter, and by raising some questions about the judgments of his readers. His answer to their charge betrays a little of his understanding of the place of self-abasement in the life of a Christian leader, something of his sense of strategy in financial decisions, and more of his love and irony.

1. The apostle's willing self-abasement (11:7). "Was it a sin," Paul asks, "for me to lower myself in order to elevate you by preaching the gospel of God to you free of charge?" Of course Paul has the right to charge for his work, to be supported by his converts (cf. 1 Cor 9:7-12a); but is it a sin if he waives his rights (cf. 12b-18)? Can it be that self-denial, the refusal to stand on agreed rights, is an offense? Is it possible that acceptance of remuneration is a realistic criterion for apostolicity?

God forbid! At least Paul's approach to money made it impossible for anyone in Corinth to think he was peddling the word of God for profit (2 Cor 2:17). Moreover, the provocative question Paul is asking displays two further elements of his self-understanding in this matter. *First,* at least part of his purpose in lowering himself by turning to manual labor while ministering to the Corinthians (cf. Acts 18:3) was to elevate them above their idolatry and immorality. When Paul first arrived in Corinth, there was no church there to support him. Not until financial help came from the already established churches in Macedonia could Paul devote his full energy to evangelism and church planting (Acts 18:5). But the lack did not force him to suspend operations until he was properly supported. His burning desire was to elevate the Corinthians by preaching the gospel; and if that meant lowering himself by manual labor for a time, Paul was up to the challenge. Far from being too proud, the apostle's love for lost men, his eagerness to raise them in Christ Jesus, the solemn imperative he felt to preach the gospel, left him with little choice but the self-abasement implicit in a teacher's turning to manual labor. The inevitable conclusion is that if the Corinthians fail to grasp Paul's purpose and follow the artificial pagan criteria of what makes a teacher great, they are simultaneously depreciating their own salvation and rejecting the love of an apostle who was willing to lower himself in order to elevate them.

But there is a *second* element. It is difficult not to see behind Paul's question a profound understanding of Christianity's central Christology: the eternal Son of God was willing to humble himself for the sake of fallen humankind, become a man himself, assume the role of a servant, and die the shameful, painful death of a convicted criminal. Paul's apostolic ministry is in some measure modeled after Christ: he writes elsewhere, "So then, death is at work in us, but life is at work in you" (2 Cor 4:12). If Christ died, it is that "those who live should no longer live for themselves but for him who died for them and was raised again" (v. 15; see esp. 6:3-10). If self-abasement is wrong in Paul, what shall be said about Jesus Christ himself? "For you know the grace of our Lord Jesus Christ, that though he was rich, yet for your sakes he became poor, so that you through his poverty might become rich" (8:9).

Here is the heart of the issue. If Paul is so wrong, presumably Christ himself was wrong. If the path of self-humiliation for the sake of others was right for Christ, and indeed central to the very nature of the gospel, why was it wrong for Paul to preach this gospel of God in a way characterized by willing self-abasement? The triumphalism being espoused by the Corinthians, Paul perceives, is not only dangerous as far as their relationship to him is concerned, but is fundamentally antithetical to the gospel itself.

There is the great dilemma and intrinsic weakness of all triumphalism: it removes itself progressively from the gospel and from Christ Jesus himself, and is more at home in an atmosphere of showmanship, one-upmanship, superstars, conquests, victories, and heroes than it is with self-sacrifice lived under the shadow of the cross. Again and again the church must ask itself how much of contemporary pagan triumphalism has been unwittingly absorbed into its life, seriously affecting the way we look at finances, service, leadership, goals, sacrifice, expectations, and even theology itself. Throughout these chapters Paul constantly sets these two structures of thought—triumphalism and biblical Christianity—over against one another in sharply etched contrasts. "Christ's pure Gospel without price and the corrupted doctrine of the Judaizers at a cost (11:20); his self-abasement and their self-glorification; his emancipation and their enslaving of the community, are pointed contrasts" (Waite).

2. The apostle's strategy (11:8-9). Paul outlines his strategy in two parts. *First,* he says, "I robbed other churches by receiving support from them so as to serve you." More explicitly, when he was in need while serving in Corinth, he did not become a burden to any Corinthian, "for the brothers who came from Macedonia" supplied what he needed (2 Cor 11:9a; Acts 18:5; Phil 4:15). It appears from this and other passages in Paul, that on occasion Paul would not only refuse all support (1 Cor 9:15-18), but that when he did receive support it was never from the church in which he was then ministering. He not only received, but could actually solicit help from churches when it was for the purpose of financing his further missionary enterprises (Acts 15:3; Rom 15:24; the expression "to send on their way" or "to help on their way" signifies financial assistance). Indeed, at one point he was prepared to receive such help from the Corinthians themselves (1 Cor 16:6,11; 2 Cor 1:16). To use Paul's expression, he "robbed" other churches to support his current ministry—which, of course, does not mean that he took their money without their consent, but that when he received it he was not rendering them a service; and in some cases, at least, the congregation could ill afford to be so generous.

Why Paul followed this pattern is nowhere clearly stated. It may have been part of his plan to preach the gospel free of charge (1 Cor 9:15-18), to proclaim, both by his message and his actions, the wonderful grace of God. People have a hard time grasping the freeness of grace: perhaps a little modeling would help. Meanwhile, the donor church, in which Paul was no longer ministering, would be learning a slightly different lesson, viz., the debt to all men under which grace places us and the privilege of sharing, by fiscal means, in the evangelization and church planting that are the responsibilities of all Christians. In neither case is Paul being remunerated for services rendered.

As far as the Corinthians are concerned, however, Paul's strategy now has a *second* part: "I have kept myself from being a burden to you in any way, and will continue to do so" (2 Cor 11:8b). It appears, then, that however willing he was in principle, at least in the past, to receive help from them toward his apostolic ministry, he is no longer willing to receive any help whatsoever from them. Of course, he will still happily collect money from them for others, e.g., for the relief of the poor in Jerusalem (2 Cor 8-9); but not one penny will he accept from them for himself.

Part of the reason for this step soon becomes explicit (2 Cor 11:12; see below). In addition, this shaping of an individual policy for the Corinthians may have been prompted by their peculiarly pagan view of remuneration. As long as they were going to weigh him by the size of his take, as long as they were utilizing the standards of the world to evaluate message and messenger alike, so long was Paul unwilling to reinforce their pagan approach by receiving anything from their hand.

3. The apostle's love (11:10-11). "As surely as the truth of Christ is in me," Paul writes—an oath taken to convince the Corinthians of the truth of what he is about to say—"nobody in the regions of Achaia, the southern half of modern Greece, where Corinth is located will stop this boasting of mine." This boasting of mine? Yes, "boasting" is the word Paul wants; for what the Corinthians see as solid evidence for Paul's insignificance, he himself understands as the crowning feature of life lived under the sign of the cross. He has no intention of reversing the policy set out in 2 Corinthians 11:7 (and 1 Cor 9:18); and far from apologizing for it or slanting away from it, he boasts in the principle of self-sacrifice that is at stake, just as later in this letter he will boast in his weakness (12:7-10).

But this boasting is not prompted by stubborn arrogance or by a haughty refusal to consider the feelings of others, still less by a kind of inverted pride in the quantity of self-sacrifice he can squeeze out of his life. As Christ's self-humiliation was prompted by the most profound love for those he came to serve, so also is Paul's. "Why," he asks his readers in effect, "do I adamantly refuse to change this policy?" Then he provides his own answer: "Because I do not love you? God knows I do!."

How deeply warped had the thinking of the Corinthians become! They have to be persuaded, under a second solemn oath ("God knows"), that the man who has readily sacrificed so much for them really loves them. Their blindness is the more surprising when we remember that Paul is simply mirroring the self-abnegation of Christ who by his poverty made others rich. Small wonder Paul begins to wonder a little whether the Corinthians are Christians at all (2 Cor 13:5). But perhaps in one sense it is not too surprising if Paul's motives and actions on this point are misunderstood; "humility and self-sacrifice often are, especially by those who do not frequently practise them" (Barrett).

4. The apostle's insightful irony (11:12). Paul understands human nature well enough to know that if the false apostles are constantly putting him down it is in part because they are envious of him and his effective ministry. If they constantly parade their alleged superiority, chances are very good they are aware of their pathetic inferiority and are trying to mask it. Paul therefore throws down the gauntlet: he will maintain his present financial policies, he says, "in order to cut the ground from under those who want an opportunity to be considered equal with us in the things they boast about."

Strictly speaking, this is not (as Barrett rightly points out) a logically effective argument. The intruders are envious of Paul's stature and effectiveness; but they quite specifically disavow his financial principles, and even lampoon them. Why should they therefore try to copy Paul in this regard?

Nevertheless, Paul's argument is psychologically effective; for it exposes the intruders as moneygrubbers, not humble and self-sacrificing leaders intent on the Corinthians' well-being. Moreover, even if the argument is not logically effective on the premises of Paul's opponents, it is on Paul's own premises; and that is just the point. If the intruders cannot follow Paul's example in these matters, it is precisely because their grasp of the gospel is pathetically defective; and therefore their boasts are worse than worthless. If they *were* to follow Paul's practice, then of course they would have to abandon their worldly policy of remuneration, and something of the pagan triumphalism behind it. Either way, Paul's skillful use of irony brings the central issues to the surface and forces the Corinthians to choose.

C. The Troublemakers Exposed (11:13-15)

Throughout these verses, Paul has been overturning the false and deceptive criteria of the interlopers. Before turning to his own long-awaited boasting, he bluntly shows the conclusion to which his argument inevitably leads: the purveyors of endlessly false criteria are false to the core.

1. False apostles: the masquerade of piety (11:13). In some of the strongest language he ever uses, Paul writes: "For such men are false apostles, deceitful workmen, masquerading as apostles of Christ." The intruders present themselves as apostles of Christ; but as Paul has already shown that their Christ is not the real one (2 Cor 11:4), their self-proclaimed status as apostles of Christ must therefore be false, a mere disguise. They were never commissioned by Christ; nor do they truly preach him, still less imitate him. They are deceitful workmen who go about in full disguise as if the church were a masquerade party.

The damage such people can do is immense. The Corinthian church had earlier proved careless in moral matters (1 Cor 5); now it is careless in matters of doctrine, attitude, and leadership. The result is an entire network of leaders, nicely installed in the church, who actively work against the gospel in the name of the gospel, seduce the people to another Jesus in the name of Jesus, and in the name of greater Christian maturity instill a deadly triumphalism that renders impossible "sincere and pure devotion to Christ" (2 Cor 11:3,4).

In light of the appalling directions the church is taking because of these false apostles, it is not surprising that the apostle's language is so strong. Two and a half centuries ago, Bengel remarked that "the Indifferentism, which is so pleasant to many in the present day, was not cultivated by Paul. He was no pleasant teacher of toleration." In fact, this problem has often endangered the church. Tasker detects the same danger in the first half of the twentieth century, when he writes, "It is a mark of the shallowness of much of the religious thinking of the modern world that Menzies, writing in 1912, should find it necessary to describe verses 13-15 as 'One of the hastiest utterances in Paul's writings,' and add that 'many of the best friends of the apostle do not defend his controversial style in this passage.'" The appeal to limitless toleration—not just toleration of the other chap's right to be wrong, but toleration pushed so far one can never say that anything or anyone is wrong—presupposes the greatest evil is to hold a strong conviction that certain things are true and their contraries are false. Worse, this presupposition operates because of an antecedent presupposition: confident knowledge in religious matters is impossible. But if we hold that God has revealed himself to men, supremely in the person of his Son, but also in the words and propositions of Scripture, then however many interpretive difficulties may still afflict us, we have no right to treat as optional anything God has said. Indeed, never to say any opinion is wrong presupposes one opinion is right—viz., the one saying no opinion is wrong. Either this is illogical, or the proponent of this view really means the one certainly correct opinion is that no *other* opinion should ever be dismissed as wrong. But how has he or she attained such certain knowledge? Few opinions are less liberal and tolerant than the form of liberalism fiercely intolerant of everything but itself.

Most people are persuaded that certain opinions are wrong; and to some extent the positions we hold, self-consciously or otherwise, define themselves against the opinions we reject. The Germans have a wise saying: *"Sage mir, mit wem du streitest, und ich sage dir, wer du bist*—Tell me with whom you are fighting, and I'll tell you who you are." Fifty years ago, J. Gresham Machen used to tell his students that the most important issues are not those on which men are agreed, but those over which they fight. His insight can of course be abused to defend cheap contentiousness; but sympathetic reflection on what he is saying discovers that for many debates his analysis is exactly right.

In the Corinthian situation, Paul and his opponents agree on many central things: monotheism, the truth of the Scriptures given to that point, the messiahship of Jesus, and much more. But the things on which they disagree are, for the issue at hand, far more important; and the manner in which each side has labeled its chief opponents serves to identify the side and reveal quite a lot about it. For the intruders, the opponent is Paul; as we learn something of him, their opposition tells us quite a bit about them: what they respect and cherish, what they reject, their values, and much more. For Paul, the intruders are the opponents; as we learn something about them, his opposition tells us quite a bit about him: how strongly he is persuaded of the truth of the gospel, how deeply he is concerned for the spiritual well-being of his converts, how sharply he reprobates false teaching in the church, how much he despises self-promotion and insincere devotion to Christ. So it is also in the modern world. Endless toleration may reflect an indifference to truth; but when we oppose something, we equally expose ourselves for what we are and cherish. There is little value in opposing things for no other reason than the love of fighting; but on the other hand to oppose nothing suggests we are blind, foolish, or careless. Christians concerned to spread the gospel effectively and stabilize the church need to follow Paul's example: identify the opponent precisely, and operate from a base of passionate devotion to the truth of biblically revealed religion and concern for the lives of men and women. If we are embarrassed by the force of his denunciation, our embarrassment may only be testimony to the degree by which we have departed from the apostolic gospel.

2. False apostles: the example of Satan (11:14-15a). Paul is not surprised that the false apostles are masquerading as apostles of Christ, "for Satan himself masquerades as an angel of light. It is not surprising, then, if his servants masquerade as servants of righteousness." Here Paul not only insists that the false apostles are followers of Satan (Jesus said something similar of some who opposed him, John 8:42-47), but that their work is characterized by deception. Their work is Satanic in origin (also hinted at by the parallel drawn in 11:3), fundamentally opposed to the gospel of God; but the focus of these lines is not so much on their spiritual pedigree per se as on the deceptiveness of their attack.

No specific passage attests Satan's self-transformation into an angel of light. The thought doubtless rests on the Bible's general teaching about the great adversary: he is a deceiver through and through, and his most effective work is achieved by cunning, disguise, and false representation. "Satan does not come to us as Satan; neither does sin present itself to us as sin, but in the guise of virtue; and the teachers of error set themselves forth as the special advocates of truth" (Hodge). The Lord Jesus himself insisted that there is no truth in Satan: "When he lies, he speaks his native language, for he is a liar and the father of lies" (John 8:44). Paul recognizes that Satan operates deceitful schemes that may outwit us.

The implications ought to trouble us if our habit is to think little about the nature of sin and temptation. Most believers are not enticed into sin by the prospect of committing great evil. Far form it; they rationalize their way into committing evil by seeing in it some kind of good, or at very least by blocking out the evil dimensions. They cheat on their income tax, not because stealing and lying are gross sins, but because (they tell themselves) there is so much government waste, because government takes more than its share, because everybody is doing it, and because no one will ever know. They gossip about neighbors and friends, not out of conscious disobedience to God, but because they feel they are passing on truth, the result of mature discernment. They nurture bitterness and hate against a spouse or a fellow believer, not because they hunger to ignore the unambiguous warnings in Scripture against bitterness and hate, but because they are persuaded their emotions are not evil after all, but simply justifiable instances of righteous indignation.

Exactly the same warped motives often prevail in their doctrinal judgments. Christians will be seduced into thinking there is no hell, not because they choose to be selective about what teachings of Jesus they will accept, but because they have heard some extrapolations on the theme of God's love that not only go beyond the biblical text but also deny some other part of Scripture. They will offer generous support of heretical teachers who appear on television, not because they love heresy, but because the scoundrels on the screen talk fluently of joy, peace, triumph, experience, and of some sort of Jesus—and who can be against such things?

The point is that the archenemy is an archdeceiver. Unless we understand this, we will be pathetically gullible, sucked into various sins and blown this way and that in our doctrine. The only certain antidote is the kind of humble walk with God that is characterized by a growing and mature knowledge of the Scriptures—"growing" in that more and more biblical truth is being digested, and "mature" in that every effort is made to put into practice whatever truth is learned from the Word of God. That kind of humble listening to the mind of God will gradually transform our own minds and largely protect us from the deceit of Satan and his servants.

The sad truth about the Christians in Corinth is that they thought themselves sophisticated believers, while in reality they were so immature they became easy dupes. Paul's assessment of the Corinthians' spiritual maturity remains unchanged from what he wrote in his first canonical epistle to them: "I gave you milk, not solid food, for you were not ready for it. Indeed, you are still not ready. You are still worldly" (1 Cor 3:2-3a).

3. False apostles: the reward of deceit (11:15b). Paul's final sentence of dismissal is stunning in its stark simplicity: "Their end will be what their actions deserve."

This sentence not only looks to the final judgment and pronounces doom, but also reflects Paul's understanding of the seriousness of the false apostles' offense. Like the Galatian Judaizers who fall under the apostolic anathema (Gal 1:8,9), Paul judges the intruders at Corinth not to be Christians at all. There is no point entering into lengthy, theological discussions with them. If Paul is right, they are not only wrong, but diabolically wrong—and correspondingly doomed. Servants of Satan do not become servants of righteousness by donning a disguise. However enticing their blandishments, evil does not become good by labeling it good. The God who calls all to account has decreed,

> Woe to those who call evil good
> and good evil,
> who put darkness for light
> and light for darkness,
> who put bitter for sweet
> and sweet for bitter.

> Woe to those who are wise in their own eyes
> and clever in their own sight

> (Isa 5:20, 21)

In particular, the Lord promises special wrath on those who do damage to his church (1 Cor 3:17; cf. 2 Tim 4:1-4).

In these verses before us, Paul has overturned the false criteria of the intruders; and in a final sally, he has exposed his opponents as the false apostles they are. If the Corinthians are paying any attention to the development of his argument, they are now much less likely to misunderstand what Paul means to accomplish by the foolish boasting to which he now turns.

5

Triumphalistic Qualifications
Answering Fools According to Their Folly

2 Corinthians 11:16-33

¹⁶ I repeat: let no one take me for a fool. But if you do, then receive me just as you would a fool, so that I may do a little boasting. ¹⁷ In this self-confident boasting I am not talking as the Lord would, but as a fool. ¹⁸ Since many are boasting in the way the world does, I too will boast. ¹⁹ You gladly put up with fools since you are so wise! ²⁰ In fact, you even put up with anyone who enslaves you or exploits you or takes advantage of you or pushes himself forward or slaps you in the face. ²¹ To my shame I admit that we were too weak for that!

What anyone else dares to boast about—I am speaking as a fool—I also dare to boast about. ²² Are they Hebrews? So am I. Are they Israelites? So am I. Are they Abraham's descendants? So am I. ²³ Are they servants of Christ? (I am out of my mind to talk like this.) I am more. I have worked much harder, been in prison more frequently, been flogged more severely, and been exposed to death again and again. ²⁴ Five times I received from the Jews the forty lashes minus one. ²⁵ Three times I was beaten with rods, once I was stoned, three times I was shipwrecked, I spent a night and a day in the open sea, ²⁶ I have been constantly on the move. I have been in danger from rivers, in danger from bandits, in danger from my own countrymen, in danger from Gentiles; in danger in the city, in danger in the country, in danger at sea; and in danger from false brothers. ²⁷ I have labored and toiled and have often gone without sleep; I have known hunger and thirst and have often gone without food; I have been cold and naked. ²⁸ Besides everything else, I face daily the pressure of my concern for all the churches. ²⁹ Who is weak, and I do not feel weak? Who is led into sin, and I do not inwardly burn?

³⁰ If I must boast, I will boast of the things that show my weakness. ³¹ The God and Father of the Lord Jesus, who is to be praised forever, knows that I am not lying. ³² In Damascus the governor under King Aretas had the city of the Damascenes guarded in order to arrest me. ³³ But I was lowered in a basket from a window in the wall and slipped through his hands.

A. The Preface of a Fool (11:16-21a)

The apostle is finally ready. He is about to embark on the foolish boasting he so much despises in others. But once more he pauses. There still remains a danger that some particularly obtuse Corinthians might wittingly or unwittingly fail to discern that Paul's boasting is not the real Paul. So again, even after placing so much distance between himself and the false apostles, between his principles of conduct and theirs, he finds it necessary to warn his readers that what he is about to do is the shoddy work of a fool, not of an apostle. In short, he offers a brief preface to explain his foolishness one more time.

1. Orientation: not taking Paul's folly seriously (11:16a). "I repeat," Paul says, "Let no one take me for a fool." In most of its occurrences in the next few verses, Paul uses "fool" to refer to those who boast in ways he finds unacceptable. In other words, they are fools from his perspective as a Christian. His readers must understand, therefore, that in the boasting on which he is about to embark, he is arguing *ad hominem.* This is no reflection of the real Paul, but only of the Paul who, to preserve the Corinthian church from moral and doctrinal seduction, must answer the real fools according to their folly.

Strictly speaking, Paul has not said these words before; so his initial "I repeat" is at first glance a little strange. But it is not strange as soon as we remember the immediately preceding verse. Paul has taken great pains to distance himself from his opponents. If he views them as false apostles, deceitful workmen, and servants of Satan, then it is unlikely that by adopting their practices (in this case, boasting) he is seriously interested in emulating them! From Christ's perspective, and therefore from Paul's, they remain fools. The apostle has already shown the unbridgeable gulf between the two. Now he "repeats" it: "Let no one take me for a fool"—i.e., let no one lump me with the false apostles because of the course I must temporarily take.

2. Apology: putting up temporarily with Paul's folly (11: 16b-18). Strictly speaking, if the Corinthians heeded Paul's initial admonition not to take him as a fool, it would only be because they have come to their senses. But Paul recognizes they are more likely to take him as a fool—i.e., both to lump him with the false apostles and to use the same wretched and inadequate criteria. But Paul can use their insensitivity: "But if you do take me for a fool," Paul writes, "then receive me just as you would a fool, so that I may do a little boasting." If the Corinthians receive him just as they would a fool, then of course they will receive Paul just as they have received the rival apostles; and such acceptance is all Paul needs to get past their mental barriers and show that, even on the basis of his rivals' criteria, he is not a bit inferior.

But having gone so far, Paul backs off. He feels intensely uncomfortable to be writing this way, to be contemplating his own enunciation of a long list of boasts. So once again he protests: "In this self-confident boasting I am not talking as the Lord would, but as a fool" (2 Cor 11:7). Paul's deep desire is to imitate Christ, even in his speech; and he knows full well that arrogant boasting was never the Lord's style. Although no one ever made higher claims for himself than did Jesus, he uttered those claims not as a mortal vainly striving for equality with

God, but as the self-emptied Son bent on the business of bringing salvation to condemned sinners. If the Lord Jesus Christ never spoke boastfully during the days of his flesh, it is outrageous to think his spirit prompts his disciples to do so today. "No boasting could ever be said to be the fruit of the Spirit!" (Tasker). Paul is painfully aware of this; and so he draws attention to the fact that what he is about to say is far removed from "the meekness and gentleness of Christ" (10:1), indeed nothing short of temporary folly. The fact remains that, as the situation stands at Corinth, Paul has very little choice: "Since many are boasting in the way the world does, I too will boast" (11:18). In other words, Paul is about to boast, not because he is following the example of Christ, but because pastoral problems in Corinth force him, temporarily, to follow the example of his opponents. The Corinthian believers have been satiated by the constant self-promotion of the interloping apostles. Either they were many in number, or the practices of relatively few had corrupted many more in the congregation. Whatever the case, Paul needed to stoop to their level for a few minutes in order to gain a hearing and put an end to the libelous accusations. Once again Paul has given his apology for inviting the Corinthians to put up temporarily with his folly.

3. Denunciation: scathing mockery of the Corinthians' wisdom (11:19-21a).

Paul has focused much of his attention on the false apostles. Here he leaves them for a moment and turns to the Corinthians themselves; and his tone becomes ironical, even scathing, as he tries to make them see that their vaunted tolerance has enslaved them, their proud wisdom has proved to be folly, their blind acceptance of the intruders and their false criteria have resulted in pain and despoliation of their substance.

Paul has been asking the Corinthians to put up with him as they would fools. Now he writes, in deeply ironical vein, "You gladly put up with fools, since you are so wise!" (2 Cor 11:19). The word "fools" in this sentence could be taken one of two ways. First, it is just possible the Corinthians have so preened themselves over their wisdom that they have regarded their father in Christ as a fool. In that case "fools" refers to those whom the proud Corinthians label thus, even if they be apostles. But because every other use of "fool" or "fools" in the immediately surrounding verses refers to those whom Paul labels fools, it is better to take this occurrence the same way. In that case, Paul is saying in effect, "You believe yourselves to be so wise, so mature, so discerning; you have been flattered into thinking you are a cut above other believers. But look at yourselves realistically: in your great wisdom you have reduced yourselves to the point where you take for your leaders such fools as the false apostles!" So, e.g., Massie: "Foolish are these boasters; but you plume yourselves on your shrewdness in accepting them. So you will, I am sure, accept me when I talk like them." This interpretation certainly makes sense of the next two verses (20-21a), as we shall see. (See also similar discussion at 11:1, in chap. 4 of this book.)

Either way, it is unconscionable that a group of Christians should view themselves as so superior to their fellow believers that they are blind to their own lack of discernment and of true wisdom. Sad to tell, this arrogance seems to have characterized many Corinthian believers; for in a passage no less ironic than this one, Paul felt compelled to write in his first canonical epistle to them, "We are fools for Christ, but you are so wise in Christ! We are weak, but you are strong! You are honored, we are dishonored!" (1 Cor 4:10).

The truth is that their self-assured wisdom bred in them a tolerance seemingly without limits; for Paul adds, "In fact, you even put up with anyone who enslaves you or exploits you or takes advantage of you or pushes himself forward or slaps you in the face" (11:20). They have not only received these leaders at face value, they have permitted them to move into positions of influence and leadership and to take over the life of the community. The intruders had become tyrants, and the Corinthians slaves—slaves not least in the servitude to new rules and criteria that detracted from God's free grace (cf. Gal 2:4; 5:1). The false apostles had exploited the congregation for tidy sums, pushed themselves forward so successfully that the local Corinthian leadership was intimidated and had been handed bruising insults (the clause "slaps you in the face" is almost certainly metaphorical language to refer to any kind of humiliating treatment).

Doubtless many Corinthians, already too impressed with worldly notions of power, felt that the brutal authority exercised by these intruding "apostles" in some sense authenticated their claims. "The Corinthians were not the last Christians to find ecclesiastical pomp and circumstance impressive. Grovelling submission to it is hardly less evil than the original arrogance" (Barrett). These dupes of triumphalism have been trampled by it. Failing to discern the profound distinctions between the lordly authority of the intruders and the self-sacrificing devotion and Spirit-entrusted authority of the apostle, they chose exploiters as their leaders and models, and blindly reveled in their own wisdom. Paul does not even want to be compared with such power-hungry exploiters. With biting irony, he contemplates their abuse of power and writes, "To my shame I admit that we were too weak for that!" (2 Cor 11:21a).

The Corinthian believers could not avoid wincing before this scathing denunciation of the wisdom of which they were so proud. They see themselves as mature and wise Christians, farsighted followers of the Savior. Yet this Savior's conduct was characterized by meekness and gentleness (cf. Matt 11:29), while here they are, kowtowing to the harsh aggressiveness and the abuse of authority exercised by servants of Satan masquerading as self-promoted apostles of Christ (2 Cor 11:13-15). Meanwhile the Corinthians enjoy despising their father in Christ because they are unimpressed by what they dismiss as "weakness," but which is nothing less than the devoted considerateness and kindness of a true apostle interested only in building them up.

Clearly Paul is fed up. Nevertheless this scathing denunciation of the Corinthians' wisdom is quite different from his ruthless exposure of the false apostles (2 Cor 11:13-15). When he rounds on the intruders, he offers no quarter and says they are not Christians at all. His irony to the Corinthians, by contrast, is striking enough to shake them out of their complacency, yet is formally very gentle: he is agreeing with them that he is weaker than the false apostles! Here is a leader with enormous pastoral sensitivity, an apostle whose diagnosis is so sensitive that he knows just what remedies to apply. The wound to the Corinthians' ego, like the wound of the surgeon, is designed to remove a particularly vicious cancer. Few malignancies are more dangerous than arrogance fed by ignorance, or triumphalism nurtured by a secular mind.

B. Apostolic Boasting (11:21b-33)

1. Paul is in no way inferior (11:12b). Several times Paul has announced that his boasting is about to begin (2 Cor 10:8; 11:1,6,16). Now, at last, it does. He opens up with a general declaration that he is in no way inferior to any conceivable rival the Corinthians may care to advance: "What anyone else dares to boast about . . . I also dare to boast about" (v. 21b). But to pen such a statement remains utterly detestable to Paul; so even now that his boasting has begun, he reminds his readers yet again in an embarrassed aside, "I am speaking as a fool."

2. Paul is heir to old covenant blessings (11:22). That Paul is not boasting abstractly, but in the concrete situation where he must compare himself with the false apostles, is made clear by the repeated "they": Are they this, or are they that?"

Paul asks three questions, all having to do with a person's relationship to the Old Testament. "Are they Hebrews?" he asks; and adds, "So am I." This means something more than that both Paul and his rivals are Jewish. The full expression, "a Hebrew of the Hebrews" (which Paul could also apply to himself, Phil 3:5), was probably used to refer to full-blooded Jews. Unlike Timothy, for instance, whose mother was a Jewess but whose father was a Gentile (Acts 16:1), Paul was not only a Hebrew but a Hebrew of the Hebrews: his parents on both sides were Jews. But the simple expression "Hebrew" or "Hebrews" most likely refers not to the purity of the bloodlines, but to language and culture (as in Acts 6:1; NASB): both Paul and his rivals were not simply Hellenistic Jews, but Hebrew Jews—i.e., Jews fluent in the Hebrew (and/or Aramaic) language and culture. Though born in Tarsus, Paul may have been reared in Jerusalem; but reared there or not, he was thoroughly educated in Semitic thought and had put down Hebrew roots.

Again, Paul asks, "Are they Israelites?" And again he responds, "So am I." If both "Hebrew" and "Israelite" refer to nothing more than race, then of course the second question is redundant (as is the third). In fact "Israelite" suggests something more. It calls to mind the Jewish people *as the people of God*, with all the rights, privileges, and heritage that entailed. Paul's own race was the people of Israel; and he says of them elsewhere, "Theirs is the adoption as sons; theirs the divine glory, the covenants, the receiving of the law, the temple worship and the promises. Theirs are the patriarchs, and from them is traced the human ancestry of Christ, who is God over all, forever praised!" (Rom 9:4-5).

Paul raises a third question: "Are they Abraham's descendants?" And again he protests, "So am I." This is probably another way of saying that Paul, no less than his opponents, could list as many Jewish qualifications in his pedigree as any might wish. As a descendant of Abraham, he was doubtless circumcised the eighth day, and made an heir of the covenants (cf. Eph 2:11-12).

What Paul really thinks of such a heritage, as far as its usefulness in commending a person to God is concerned, comes to explicit expression in another of his epistles:

> If anyone else thinks he has reasons to put confidence in the flesh, I have more: circumcised on the eighth day, of the people of Israel, of the tribe of Benjamin, a Hebrew of Hebrews; in regard to the law, a Pharisee; as for zeal, persecuting the church; as for legalistic righteousness that comes from the law, faultless.
>
> But whatever was to my profit I now consider loss for the sake of Christ. What is more, I consider everything a loss compared to the surpassing greatness of knowing Christ Jesus my Lord, for whose sake I have lost all things. I consider them rubbish, that I may gain Christ. (Phil 3:4b-8).

But for now, he must present his pedigree to remind the Corinthians that he is no less Jewish, no less a son of Abraham, no less an heir of the covenants, no less a Jew trained in the ancient language and heritage, than any of the false apostles who oppose him. That he must put this matter first on the list of boasts (indeed, the only detailed boasts that do not partake of the biting irony characteristic of the remaining entries) strongly confirms that the intruders in the Corinthian church are Judaizers, probably from Palestine.

3. *Paul is an exemplary servant of Christ (11:23a).* Paul now turns from the old covenant to the new, from race and heritage to achievement. Moreover, he no longer restricts himself to being the equal of his opponents (e.g., "Are they Hebrews? So am I.") Rather, he insists on his superiority: "Are they servants of Christ? . . . I am more." But to write in this vein sends him into spiritual agony, and he cannot restrain himself from bursting out again, "I am out of my mind to talk like this."

Because Paul has already insisted that the false apostles are not true servants of Christ at all, several interpreters argue that those to whom Paul is referring here cannot be the same people. After all, if Paul is more of a servant of Christ than those of whom he is speaking, they themselves must be servants of Christ in *some* sense. As a result, it is argued, the people with whom Paul is comparing himself here must be the genuine apostles, the Twelve; and in hard, pioneer work, Paul *excels more* than they do (cf. 1 Cor 15:10).

But this interpretation puts an intolerable strain on the unity of the passage. 2 Corinthians 13-15 unambiguously refer to the intruders, the false apostles. When Paul continues in vv. 16-21a, he must still be talking about the same group, not about the Twelve; for he writes of those "who are boasting in the way the world does" and who exploit and humiliate the Corinthians. Immediately after this paragraph, Paul says that "what anyone else dares to boast about" he can boast about too. The natural way to take this is as a continued reference to the worldly boasters, the false apostles. Why else speak of *daring* to boast? Moreover Paul insists his boasting is not Christian speech but the talk of a fool. If the others who dare to boast are the Twelve, Paul is implicitly labeling all of them fools—which is singularly unlikely. It is much better to allow the natural reading of the passage to stand: i.e., Paul is still referring to the intruders. The word "they" in the following sentences follows on as a reference to the same false apostles, for there is no convenient break at verse 23 to suggest Paul is switching subjects from the deceitful workmen to the Twelve.[1]

What then shall we make of Paul's question and answer, "Are they servants of Christ? . . . I am more"? Does he really think, after the unrelenting condemnation of 2 Corinthians 11:13-15, that the false apostles are not so false after all, but are truly servants of Christ, even if poor ones? No, of course not; but such

---

1. In the last few decades, there has been an enormous amount of work aimed at identifying Paul's opponents here and in other epistles. The subject is too intricate and the results too tentative to be probed in a profitable way here, beyond the sketch of the one alternative position I have tried to refute above and in chapter 1.

an interpretation pushes the language of Paul's question and answer beyond reasonable boundaries. In this context, the question "Are they servants of Christ?" really means "Do they claim to be servants of Christ" or, better yet, "Are they servants of Christ [according to the criteria you Corinthians have been taught to use]?" For that is just Paul's point: by whatever criteria, Paul is *more* of a servant of Christ than they—even if the criteria are finally shown to be outrageously sub-Christian. There is no contradiction between verses 13 and 23. The former verse tells us what Paul really thinks of the intruders, and the latter what the Corinthians think of them. This makes Paul's agonizing parenthesis perfectly understandable: precisely because he does not want to be compared with the false apostles and their proud, man-centered boasting in any way, he writes, "I am out of my mind to be talking like this!"

4. Superb irony: the overthrow of all categories for boasting used by triumphalists (11:23b-29). According to the logic of the situation, Paul should now go on to show in what ways he is a superior servant of Christ. Indeed, he appears on the verge of such boasting, for he says, "I have worked much harder." This may simply be a fair description of Paul's labors, so well attested in Acts, as compared with the limited efforts of the interlopers. The clause may also reflect the fact that Paul on occasion worked hard with his own hands. But above all, these words raise our expectations as to what must follow. We might imagine Paul saying something like this: "I have established more churches; I have preached the gospel in more lands and to more ethnic groups; I have traveled more miles; I have won more converts; I have written more books; I have raised more money; I have dominated more councils; I have walked with God more fervently and seen more visions; I have commanded the greatest crowds and performed the most spectacular miracles." After all, that is the sort of list many pagans actually did produce, albeit with different entries. There was even a kind of stylized way of writing up such a brag-sheet, a technique modern scholars refer to as "well known encomiastic conventions." Augustus Caesar, for instance, wrote an eulogy in his own honor, an encomium that listed his many accomplishments (the so-called *Res gestae Divi Augusti*). Augustus is careful to include numbers: once I did this,

three times I did that, many times the other. It is highly probable
Paul himself had read Caesar's *Res Gestae* since it was inscribed
on monuments in many of the provinces. Other lists of self-praise
are common in the Graeco-Roman world and fit very nicely with
the prevailing attitudes toward self-promotion that I have already
outlined. Thus, Paul follows the accepted pattern, even to the
point of using the numbers that were an important part of these
self-eulogies (five times I was flogged, three times shipwrecked,
etc.). "But even a superficial comparison between Paul's catalogue
of his sufferings and Augustus' and Pompey's whitewashed
accounts of their glorious achievements shows that Paul's
catalogue is a carefully calculated *reductio ad absurdum* [a re-
duction of the argument to absurdity] of the whole Graeco-
Roman attitude to boasting" (Travis, p. 530, n. 1).

Instead of talking about his exploits and his victories, Paul
details his sufferings, loss, shame, and defeats. It is almost as if
the primary (if not the only) incontestable criterion of true
apostleship is massive suffering in the service of Christ (cf. 1 Cor
4:9-13; 2 Cor 4:7-12; 6:4,5). There is very little for triumphalists
to say once Paul has finished. The systems of values espoused
by Paul and his opponents are so diametrically antithetical that
there remains very little common ground.

I shall reflect a little further on the significance of this list
later; but it is worth our while first to pause briefly at each entry.

Been in prison more frequently: This epistle was written about
the time of travel described in Acts 20:2a; and before that period,
Acts records only one imprisonment, viz., the one that took place
in Philippi (Acts 16:23-40). Imprisonment in Jerusalem, Caesarea,
and Rome all took place later. It is just possible the apostle spent
time in jail during his Ephesian ministry (cf. 1 Cor 15:32; 2 Cor
1:8-9). A document written at the end of the first century says
Paul was in prison on seven different occasions (1 Clement 5:6),
but it may have been much more. Two things are already clear.
First, the Book of Acts does not give us anything like a full
account of Paul's sufferings. Even at this intermediate stage of
his apostolic career, Paul had been in prison "many times"
unmentioned by Luke. Second, the false apostles would not have
chosen this as a lead item in their resume. Paul has already
begun the scathing irony.

Been flogged more severely: If prison was shameful, flogging was both shameful and painful, and could inflict mortal wounds. This generic word "flogging" receives more detailed breakdown in the next two verses. The word translated "more severely" does not suggest that Paul was beaten "more severely" than the false apostles, who were therefore (it might be concluded) beaten less severely. Rather, it means Paul was beaten "beyond measure."

Been exposed to death again and again: Like the last entry, this clause refers in general terms to many different kinds of situations in which there was mortal danger, situations detailed in the following verses. "When the apostle would prove himself an *extraordinary minister,* he proves that he had been an extraordinary sufferer. . . . The jail and the whipping-post, and all the other hard usages of those who are accounted the worst of men, were what he was accustomed to" (Henry).

Five times I received from the Jews the forty lashes minus one (11:24): Jesus predicted that opponents of his gospel would hand his disciples over to the local councils and flog them in their synagogues (Matt 10:17). None of these scourgings by Paul's Jewish compatriots is recorded in Acts. That Paul faced this ordeal five times by this point in his ministry is profound testimony to his persistent attempts to reach his fellow Jews with the gospel (cf. Rom 1:16b; 9:1-4a; 10:1). Never did he restrict himself to Gentiles only. These Jewish beatings were probably mandated by the local court attached to many synagogues to dispense justice among the Jews of the community.

Why was Paul beaten? A passage in the Mishnah provides a long list of crimes that could earn the forty lashes, including incest and certain other sexual sins, entering the Temple in an unclean condition, marring the corners of one's beard, tattooing, and breaking a Nazirite vow (Makkoth 3:1-9). Not only is it unlikely Paul was guilty of any of these crimes, but the context in 2 Corinthians 11 makes it clear that his beatings were connected with his apostolic ministry. Certainly by the third century A.D. flogging was the customary punishment for a scholar who came under the synagogue ban; and something of the sort must have happened to Paul as well. Probably there was some sort of legal excuse. The charge may have been specific: consorting with Gentiles or eating forbidden food or the like. When I was a boy, Christian ministers and evangelists spent a total of eight years in jail during 1950-1952 in Quebec, because they preached the gospel in the open air and handed out literature; but the charge was always something else, such as inciting to riot or disturbing the peace.

The beating was severe. The Old Testament limited the maximum number of lashings that a court could impose to forty; but the practice in Paul's day was to keep the limit to thirty-nine (hence his reference to "forty lashes minus one"). The medieval Jewish scholar Maimonides surmised that this was done to ensure that no officer of the court ever went over the maximum. Be that as it may, the number of lashings in Paul's day had to be divisible by the number three, because the scourge used had three thongs, the central one of calf-hide and the other two of ass-hide. One blow, therefore, administered three stripes; and the maximum number of blows was thirteen (3 x 13 = 39). Fewer might be given if the court felt that the prisoner might not survive the full quota. If Paul five times received the full thirty-nine lashes, "there is no occasion for taking into account bodily weakness in the case of Paul" (Meyer): he must have been physically very tough and resilient, for such flogging could kill a man. It took place by binding the prisoner's arms, as he lay on his back, to two pillars, one on either side. The minister of the synagogue then tore open the prisoner's clothes, baring his chest. One third of the blows were then administered, the whip ends long enough to extend from the prisoner's shoulder to his navel. The prisoner was then released, rolled over, tied down again; and the remaining two thirds of the prescribed number of blows was administered to his back. "And he that smites, smites with his one hand with all his might" (Makkoth 3:13).

Three times I was beaten with rods (11:25): This is almost certainly a reference to Roman beatings, not Jewish. Acts records only one of these (Acts 16:22-23). There was no limit to the number of blows; and they could be landed anywhere on the prisoner's body, which was stripped naked in preparation. In theory, this punishment (often used in connection with interrogating a suspect) was not to be inflicted on any Roman citizen (cf. Acts 16:37; 22:25,29; Cicero, *In Verrem* v.170: "To bind a Roman citizen is a crime, to flog him is an abomination.") Yet there is ample evidence that in Paul's day this breach of law occurred rather frequently (Cicero, *In Verrem* 5.161-62; Livy, 10.9.3-6). The charge brought against Paul was probably disturbing the peace. In any event, no triumphalist would confess he had run afoul of the Roman judicial system. The shame of these public beatings was matched only by the agony they inflicted.

Once I was stoned (11:25): Doubtless this is a reference to Paul's horrifying experience in Lystra (Acts 14:19) where he was roughly handled by a mob, stoned, and left for dead. There was no legal procedure in this case, of course (as under the judical stoning of a Jewish court: cf. *Sanhedrin* 6:1-6), but only mob violence. From the perspective of the person being stoned, however, it is very doubtful that stones would feel any different if they had been hurled only after proper procedure had taken place.

Three times I was shipwrecked (11:25): These words Paul wrote *before* the shipwreck recorded in Acts 27. So Paul must have survived at least four such terrifying experiences in his life. We do not know when the earlier three took place. One or more may have occurred in connection with the travels of his first or second missionary journeys (sea voyages are mentioned in Acts 13:4,13; 14:26; 16:11; 17:5; 18:18; and there were certainly other sea trips, e.g., 2 Cor 2:1,13; 7:5); or perhaps they all took place in the silent years of ministry before his arrival in Antioch to work with Barnabas.

I spent a night and a day in the open sea (11:25): One of the shipwrecks, at least, proved very dangerous. Apparently it occurred far enough from land that the distance was too great to swim, and Paul was left in the water, clinging to wreckage perhaps, until rescue arrived.

I have been constantly on the move (11:26): In some ways this is a transitional statement introducing the specific dangers enumerated in the following lines. But perhaps it also hints at something of the privation that most people feel if they are on the road constantly, with no place truly home.

I have been in danger from rivers, in danger from bandits (11:26): Both dangers would be occasioned by the apostle's many travels. Some rivers would be dangerous to ford at any time, others at certain times of the year. Highwaymen infested some parts of the empire more thickly than others. Both rivers and bandits were particularly dangerous for the traveler who tried to cross the Taurus Mountains between Perga in Pamphylia and Pisidian Antioch in Phrygia (Acts 13:14; 14:24). The danger of robbers might be particularly bad when Paul was carrying money from one church to another for the relief of the poor.

In danger from my own countrymen (11:26): Much of the earliest persecution of the church came from the Jewish side. The Book of Acts tells of several Jewish plots against Paul's life (e.g., Acts 9:23,29: 13:45: 14:2,19: 15:26; 17:5ff.; 18:1,12).

In danger from Gentiles (11:26): Acts recounts three such episodes (14:19-20, at Jewish instigation; 16:16-40; 19:23-41).

In danger in the city, in danger in the country, in danger at sea (11:26): Paul now moves from the human origins of his dangers to their geographical locations. The three-fold string, cities/country/sea, leaves very little left: in other words, Paul is in danger everywhere, all the time. Moreover, in the context of the seriousness of the charge, the danger Paul confronts is probably to life and limb: it is not mere irritation. Crowded city made dangerous by endless plots against him, bandit-infested countryside, and the potential for shipwrecks might have deterred a lesser man from his ministry, but not Paul.

And in danger from false brothers (11:26): "Brothers" means "fellow-Christians"; so "false brothers" probably means those who claim to be fellow-Christians but are not. There is an unmistakable reference back to false apostles (2 Cor 11:13). Most such false brothers in Paul's day would be Judaizers. They would easily pass for Christians and be acceptable in most churches, for they certainly believed Jesus to be the Messiah, and that he died and rose again. But because they insisted that Gentiles must in some respects come under the law of Moses, as well as bow to the lordship of Jesus Messiah in repentance and faith if they were to be saved at all, they found themselves in direct conflict with the apostolic gospel, which insisted no less strongly on the *exclusive sufficiency* of Jesus Christ. In Jerusalem, the issue would not have been as burning as in the provinces (unless someone like Paul brought the matter up), because there were very few Gentiles there. This made Paul the focus of Judaizing opposition, for his ministry was primarily exercised among Gentiles.

Probably on occasion the apostle was betrayed by some Jewish leaders into the hands of local authorities and thereby met with various reprisals, direct and indirect. At the same time, Paul's listing of false brothers as one of his great dangers and sources of suffering, along with flogging, shipwrecks, and stoning could only be a stinging rebuke to the Corinthians themselves; for if they had not harbored the rival apostles and given them a secure base and a sympathetic ear, Paul would not have needed to write this response at all. Duped brothers often multiply the evil influence of false brothers.

I have labored and toiled and have often gone without sleep (11:27): Quite apart from the extraordinary dangers and all too frequent beatings and imprisonments that the apostle faced during the course of his ministry, his life was scarcely characterized by luxury, comfort, reflective ease, or even much rest (cf. 1 Cor 4:9-13,24-27; 2 Cor 6:4-10). He "labored" and "toiled" (a pair of verbs Paul has used elsewhere to describe his combination of spiritual ministry and manual work, 1 Thess 2:9; 2 Thess 3:8). Both words suggest not only the energy that went into the work itself, but the resulting fatigue and accompanying hardship as well. In this context, the sleeplessness is probably due neither to easy choice nor to insomnia, but to the pressures of too much work and too many responsibilities.

I have known hunger and thirst and have often gone without food; I have been cold and naked (11:27): It is unlikely that the bouts of hunger came from self-imposed fasts connected with Christian festivals or private hours of prayer; for if Paul could bring himself to mention such fasts, he certainly would not do so in a list of sufferings and privations. Far more likely is the suggestion that Paul experienced hunger and thirst associated with awkward travel arrangements and with an empty pocketbook. Paul determined not to accept support from the Corinthians (1 Cor 9:12,15,18; 2 Cor 11:7-12; 12:14-16a); and this may well have precipitated one of the periods of hunger. Cold and nakedness might be forced on him either by prison life or, again, by financial destitution. While the Corinthians were being taught that truly great teachers earned huge fees and commanded multiplying assets, the apostle Paul frequently lived so far below the poverty line he would have needed substantial sums to reach it. For this he suffered doubly: the privations themselves, and then the condescending scorn of immature triumphalists who married pagan greed with over-realized eschatology to argue that financial prosperity was the reward of the just and the right of sons of God, conveniently forgetting the cross.

"Besides everything else," Paul writes (the expression could mean "besides all the other things left unmentioned," or "besides all I've mentioned and more of the same," or, less likely, "besides external trials"), "I face daily the pressure of my concern for all the churches" (2 Cor 11:28). Here is Paul the pastor and world Christian. His concern extends to all the churches, doubtless first and foremost the ones he himself founded, but not limited to that boundary, since Paul often uses the plural "churches" to refer to the whole people of God (e.g., Rom 16:16; 1 Cor 7:17; 11:16; 14:33; 2 Cor 8:18; 2 Thess 1:4). The epistles to the Romans and to the Colossians were written to churches Paul had neither founded nor visited; but that fact did not prevent him from expressing profound concern for the churches in Rome and Colosse.

The concern Paul felt is no violation of Jesus' prohibition of self-interested worry (Matt 6:25-34); for the worry Jesus forbids is set over against seeking first God's kingdom and righteousness, the very virtue Paul's concern for the churches most deeply displays.[2] While the rival apostles compromise themselves by seeking power, money, and fame; Paul seeks none of the three. He preaches the kingdom of God and teaches about the Lord Jesus Christ (Acts 28:31), and is passionately concerned for righteousness (as 2 Cor 11:29 proves).

Paul seems to view his concern for all the churches as the climax of his trials. The immensity of the pressures and sufferings already enumerated therefore serve as a measure of the intensity of his care for fellow believers. Certainly if many congregations had problems as serious as those in Galatia and Corinth, Paul must have poured staggering quantities of emotional and spiritual energy into the churches he loved so well. If Paul faces such pressure daily, it is not because a bad situation never improves, but because there is always a new one about to break. Nor is Paul's concern limited to churches that are in danger of apostasizing. He cares with equal intensity for fledgling congregations he is not in a position to help directly, but the newness of whose faith prompts the apostle to vigilant prayer and whatever is the spiritual equivalent of gnawed fingernails.

The church in Thessalonica, for instance, came into existence as a result of apostolic work that spanned at most a few weeks;

---

2. I have dealt a little more comprehensively with Jesus' teaching on worry in *The Sermon on the Mount* (Grand Rapids: Baker, 1978) pp. 81-96.

and Paul's first epistle back to them reflects, not only the tenderest love, but a doting parent's unqualified concern (see esp. 1 Thess 1:4-3:10). Forced in this instance to remain at a distance, Paul makes a decision: "So when we could stand it no longer, we thought it best to be left by ourselves in Athens. We sent Timothy, who is our brother and God's fellow worker in spreading the gospel of Christ, to strengthen and encourage you in your faith, so that no one would be unsettled by these trials. . . . Timothy has just now come to us from you and has brought good news about your faith and love. . . . Therefore, brothers, in all our distress and persecution we were encouraged about you because of your faith. For now we really live, since you are standing firm in the Lord. . . . Night and day we pray most earnestly that we may see you again and supply what is lacking in your faith" (3:1-10).

Here is no mere professional, running a superb organization from the comfort of a well-appointed, air-conditioned office, but a pastor attuned to the needs of even the least brother for whom Christ died. Organization and competent administration there are, as a close study of the comings and goings of Paul's numerous assistants reveals; nevertheless, this apostolic ministry is not discharged with aloof detachment, but with flaming zeal, profound compassion, evangelistic fervor, and a father's heart. Paul engages all his considerable intellectual and emotional power in his ministry to the whole church. Such an approach bears fruit; but it takes its toll in energy consumed and in deep involvement with people.

This is brought to sharp focus as Paul provides an example, set forth by a couple of rhetorical questions: "Who is weak, and I do not feel weak? Who is led into sin, and I do not inwardly burn?" (2 Cor 11:29). "Weakness" in the Pauline corpus can refer to personal faith or conscience: i.e., a believer whose faith or conscience is weak may suffer pangs of false guilt and observe regulations of indifferent importance (e.g., Rom 4:9; 14:1,2; 1 Cor 8:11-12). But in this context "weakness" probably bears its broader sense, referring to lack of strength in any respect. Paul is talking about Christians who for some reason have been brought to a spiritual low point, and who seem to have no reserves of strength to overcome temptation, doubt, seduction, and opposition, or to get on with the business of discipleship.

Paul empathizes deeply, for he has frequently experienced the most debilitating weakness, including illness (Gal 4:13), discouragement, and fear (Acts 18:9-10; 1 Cor 2:3), and the perpetual pressures generated by the list of apostolic "credentials" he is now bringing to a close (cf. also 2 Cor 4:7-12). How could triumphalists who boast only of their strength and who despise all signs of weakness ever provide any empathetic help to the fellow believer who is weak?

No less acute is the intensity of his feeling when a Christian is led into sin.[3] Paul cannot stoop to indifference when any believer, whether by the persuasive power of evil example, by the saccharine seduction of duplicitous personalities, or by the bane of false teaching, is tripped up and made to stumble into sin. The apostle burns inwardly, not only with the compassionate empathy presupposed by the previous question, but now also with fiery indignation against those who lead one of Christ's little ones into sin (cf. Matt 18:6; Gal 5:12). That explains the heat of Paul's reaction and the vehemence of his language in 2 Cor 11:13-15. Unreservedly committed both to the righteousness bound up with the gospel and to the brothers and sisters transformed by that gospel, Paul burns when he sees righteousness in ruins and believers morally battered by the servants of Satan.

How different are many of our reactions to the same phenomenon today. It is regrettably easy to philosophize when such sin occurs, comment on the evil times in which we live, reflect that the brother or sister who fell into sin or heresy was never very strong or discerning anyway, and never to agonize in prayer for our fellow believer or inwardly burn because of their weakness and shame. The really consistent triumphalist may actually entertain feelings of superiority in that situation, and rejoice that he is not as other men are. Our indifference

---

3. It has been argued that the verb *skandalizetai*, rendered "is led into sin" by the NIV, really means "is offended" in this context; and Paul replies in effect that when other Christians are offended he can "burn" empathetically with them, for he has frequently been offended himself. This interpretation is unlikely. Though the verb can indeed mean "is offended," this is normally not in the sense that someone has had his feelings hurt, but that some "offense" has been committed against that person. In biblical usage this "offense" often leads the victim into sin. Moreover, the "burning" Paul feels toward the offenders is contextually shaped by 11:13-15.

links us with the priest and Levite in the parable of the good
Samaritan (Luke 10:25-37).

5. Boasting of weakness and shame (11:30-33). With
magnificent irony, Paul has scathingly rejected the criteria of the
triumphalists by boasting of his sufferings, beatings, deprivations, and exhausting concerns. Now he turns the argument in
a new direction. He boasts about an event in his life of which
he is ashamed. "If I must boast," he writes (possibly echoing an
axiom of the rival apostles that one must boast), "I will boast
of the things that show my weakness." This paradoxical boasting
is the only kind of boasting the apostle can tolerate for long.

What he is about to say is, from the perspective of triumphalism, so improbable that Paul puts himself under an oath
before he begins: "The God and Father of the Lord Jesus, who
is to be praised forever, knows that I am not lying" (2 Cor 11:32).
The proper function of oaths is not to erect special situations
in which truth-telling is important, by contrast with other
situations in which truth-telling does not matter; rather, they
function to enhance the credibility of the speaker before
skeptical hearers. Paul's credibility has been questioned; he takes
this oath, appealing to God's omniscience, to ensure the
Corinthians will hear him out and be more inclined to believe
him (for other Pauline oaths cf. 2 Cor 1:18; 11:10-11; Rom 9:1;
Gal 1:20; 1 Tim 2:7).

At first glance, what he tells the Corinthians seems innocuous
enough: it is the account of his escape from Damascus. "In
Damascus the governor under King Aretas had the city of the
Damascenes guarded in order to arrest me. But I was lowered
from a basket through a window in the wall and slipped through
his hands" (2 Cor 11:32-33).

This is Paul's version of the escape described by Luke in Acts
9:23-25. It is not entirely clear why the governor tried to arrest
Paul, but probably his reason was grounded in Paul's evangelistic
activity in Arabia (Gal 1:17), the area inhabited by the Nabataean
Arabs over whom Aretas ruled. There are other historical
uncertainties;[4] but Paul's terse report is clear enough. He

---

4. Luke says the Jews were watching the gates in order to kill Paul (Acts 9:23-
25); Paul says the governor under King Aretas had the city guarded in order

escaped from the city by passing through a hatch in the wall and being lowered to the ground in a fish basket, assisted by some of his disciples.

Why should Paul tell this story with such an obvious sense of weakness and shame? Why must he put himself under oath, as if this is so hard to believe? There are two observations that will bring us to the heart of what Paul is saying in these verses.

First, many readers of the English Bible have become familiar with the escape through Sunday schools, where the story is told, not only from the perspective of Luke (who is more interested in God's providential direction of the church and preservation of this "apostle to the Gentiles" than in Paul's personal feelings), but as an adventure in which the "good guy" wins. It can actually be exciting on flannelgraph! But the good guy himself didn't look back on the event as a piece of high drama to spice up his memoirs. Rather, he recalled the event with shame. Probably it was the event that shattered whatever residual pride still lurked in the proud heart of Saul the Pharisee. He had set out for the city of Damascus with the avowed intent of rounding up Christians; he left the city not as the hunter but as the hunted. This toast of high rabbinic circles, this educated and sincere

---

to arrest him. This problem is related to uncertainty as to who was really in charge of Damascus at the time. The Romans certainly ruled the city until A.D. 34, and they may have ruled long after that; but the absence of Roman coins in Damascus for the period A.D. 34-62 has convinced some historians that King Aretas IV, father-in-law of Herod Antipas and ruler of Nabataea from about 9 B.C. to A.D. 40, extended his territory in A.D. 34 to include Damascus, and maintained oversight through a deputy while the king himself maintained his palace in Petra. If this is correct, then it is possible (as Hughes suggests) that this governor was himself a Jew (compare the connection between Aretas and the half-breed Herods) who appointed an entirely Jewish unit of guards to regulate what was in fact a purely Jewish matter. This search for Paul then becomes the first of many bouts with his Jewish compatriots. But it is marginally more likely that the Romans never relinquished control of the city. In that case the "governor" was probably an appointee of King Aretas to rule over a semi-autonomous colony of Nabataean Arabs in the city. This sort of arrangement the Romans fostered in other cities (e.g., it appears the Jews in Alexandria enjoyed long periods of semi-autonomous self-government in their section of the city); and indeed the word rendered "governor" by the NIV, *ethnarchēs,* customarily refers to a relatively minor governor over a tribal group. In this view, Paul's evangelistic activity offended the Jews of Damascus, and his forays in Arabia offended the Nabataean Arabs. The Jews (Acts) and Nabataeans (Paul) therefore forged an agreement to stop him, precipitating the escape.

Pharisee, this man who had access to the highest officials in
Jerusalem, slunk out of Damascus like a criminal, lowered like
a catch of dead fish in a basket whose smelly cargo he had
displaced. It is even possible that his detractors had held this
event up to the Corinthians as proof of Paul's cowardice (cf.
10:1,10). "What a contrast there was between his arrogant
approach to the city, and his humiliating exit from it!" (Wilson).

The *second* observation is still more telling. The list of boasts
(2 Cor 11:23-29), it will be remembered, is shaped as a parody
of the self-praise great public figures commonly wrote in their
own honor. In these last few verses, Paul parodies the type of
self-eulogy that singles out one detail and describes it graphically
as a kind of paradigm of what might be expected from such
a man. Now it becomes perfectly clear why Paul focuses
attention on a single incident partly trivial and partly shameful.

> He will boast, if he must, of his weaknesses. But if it is realised
> that everyone in antiquity would have known that the finest
> military award for valour was the *corona muralis*, for the man
> who was first up the wall in the face of the enemy, Paul's point
> is devastatingly plain: he was first down.[5]

The triumphalists are so very proud of their accomplishments,
such as they are. But while everyone is showing off his war
medals, including the odd Congressional Medal of Honor, Paul
tells how he ran away in the face of the enemy. He is determined
to boast of the things that will show his weakness. He might have
penned the following lines:

> Credentials apostolic: here's my boast,
> Certificate of God's elusive call.
> I might have pointed out that I am Paul,
> A Benjamite of purest lines, the toast
> Of high rabbinic educators, most
> Experienced church planter; but the pall
> Of guilt, the grace of God, Golgotha—all
> Combine to prompt this apostolic boast:
>   Like wretched slaves I've worked, and borne the lash.

5. E. A. Judge, "The Conflict of Educational Aims in NT Thought," *Journal
of Christian Education* 9 (1966) 45.

Severely beaten, stoned, and shipwrecked thrice,
In constant danger, treated like old trash
By my own flocks—these prove I serve the Christ.
For I delight to suffer weakness, wrong.
Grace answers need; and when I'm weak, I'm strong.[6]

C. Some Final Reflections

Comparison of this list with Luke's selective presentation of Paul's ministry shows that, far from exaggerating, Luke records only a small part of Paul's work and suffering for Jesus Christ. We would have no knowledge of the extent of Paul's labors, privations, and beatings were it not for the fact that, in the providence of God, Paul is forced to write this parody in order to save the Corinthian church; for it is quite clear the apostle would not easily have offered such information. His agony over the matter is our great gain.

It is very humbling to become intimately acquainted with a servant of Christ like Paul. But we will not be honoring him, nor worshiping the Lord he loves, if we do not reflect a little further on the appropriate application to our own lives of so moving and candid a self-portrayal.

1. Christians ought to be greatly ashamed of boasting about strengths, skills, victories, training, successes, and productivity in their lives as if, on the one hand, we either earned those things or deserved them, or as if, on the other, such things make us intrinsically more acceptable to the Lord Jesus Christ. What do we have but what we have received? And if we received it as a gracious gift from God, how dare we boast about it (1 Cor 4:7)? Does not the most elementary grasp of the gospel assure us that we are accepted by God solely by the merits of Christ Jesus the Redeemer? Why then so much boasting? Is our love of man's applause stronger than our love for Christ?

2. Christians ought to be quick to admit to their weaknesses, because rightly handled our weaknesses will serve to extol Christ's strength and therefore bring glory to him. I know a Christian leader who openly advises his colleagues never to admit their weaknesses. To do so, he says, might give opponents

6. D. A. Carson, *Sonnets from Scripture*, (forthcoming).

an advantage. Christian this leader may be; but in this respect he thinks like a pagan.

3. In any case, Christians must not uncritically drag over from the world criteria of self-assessment whose underlying values actually betray biblical discipleship to Jesus Christ. Paul's deeply ironic boasting is not the work of a man who is naturally self-effacing. Behind the lines in these verses stands an apostle who has by God's grace thought through the implications of his discipleship to the Lord Jesus, and has learned in large measure to think and act in ways consistent with that calling. His grasp of grace and his desire to imitate his Savior provide the impulse behind his boasting.

The solution to overblown self-esteem and self-eulogizing is neither an artificial self-loathing nor a valiant attempt to try harder. It is unconditional devotion to Jesus Christ. In these matters nothing will mature us more effectively than multiplied devotion to the Lord Jesus and growing, biblically controlled reflection on the entailments of our discipleship, until we can sing unreservedly:

Savior! Thy dying love
Thou gavest me;
Nor should I aught withhold,
Dear Lord, from Thee;
In love my soul would bow,
My heart fulfill its vow,
Some off'ring bring Thee now,
Something for Thee.

At the blest mercy-seat,
Pleading for me;
My feeble faith looks up,
Jesus, to Thee:
Help me the cross to bear,
Thy wondrous love declare,
Some song to raise, or prayer,
Something for Thee.

Give me a faithful heart,
Likeness to Thee,
That each departing day

Henceforth may see
Some work of love begun,
Some deed of kindness done,
Some wand'rer sought and won,
Something for Thee.

All that I am and have—
Thy gifts so free—
In joy, in grief, through life,
O Lord, for Thee!
And when Thy face I see
My ransomed soul shall be
Through all eternity
Something for Thee.

Sylvanus Dryden Phelps (1816-95)

Destroying Super-Spiritual Visionaries
Boasting in Weakness

2 Corinthians 12:1-10

¹ I must go on boasting. Although there is nothing to be gained, I will go on to visions and revelations from the Lord. ² I know a man in Christ who fourteen years ago was caught up to the third heaven. Whether it was in the body or out of the body I do not know—God knows. ³ And I know that this man—whether in the body or apart from the body I do not know, but God knows—⁴ was caught up to Paradise. He heard inexpressible things, things that man is not permitted to tell. ⁵ I will boast about a man like that, but I will not boast about myself, except about my weaknesses. ⁶ Even if I should choose to boast, I would not be a fool, because I would be speaking the truth. But I refrain, so no one will think more of me than is warranted by what I do or say.

⁷To keep me from becoming conceited because of these surpassingly great revelations, there was given me a thorn in my flesh, a messenger of Satan, to torment me. ⁸ Three times I pleaded with the Lord to take it away from me. ⁹ But he said to me, "My grace is sufficient for you, for my power is made perfect in weakness." Therefore I will boast all the more gladly about my weaknesses, so that

Christ's power may rest on me. [10] That is why, for Christ's sake, I delight in weaknesses, in insults, in hardships, in persecutions, in difficulties. For when I am weak, then I am strong.

A. More Boasting (12:1)

"I must go on boasting," Paul writes, probably in mimicry of a Corinthian slogan such as "One must boast" (cf. 2 Cor 11:30). Yet the apostle adds, "Although there is nothing to be gained, I will go on to visions and revelations from the Lord" (12:1).

Then the theme of foolish boasting continues, reaching its climax in 12:1-10. As Paul admits at the end of this boasting. "I have made a fool of myself, but you drove me to it" (v. 11). The way the Corinthians drove Paul to this particular topic for boasting is best explained by supposing that the false apostles not only claimed superiority in such things as rhetoric, eloquence, ability to command fees, leadership, and knowledge of the truth, they also claimed spiritual superiority. In support of their claims they could recount a continuing array of visions and revelations they were receiving. A confident "The Lord told me this morning..." may not only enhance one's reputation as a man or woman of God, but may prove wonderfully coercive. Few will stop to ask in what way the Lord said this or that (By an audible voice? By quiet, personal conviction? By tongues?), or point out that the authority status of such revelations in the New Testament is less than is commonly believed.[1] Fewer still will pause to remember that not every supernatural power is divine. Certainly the triumphalists won't raise questions of this sort; their first reaction will be that such questions quench the Spirit. And so the claims of spiritual prowess are paraded out, and personal authority grows with the "sharing" of each vision.

Contrast Paul, the false apostles might remark. What visions has he claimed to see in recent years? Does he talk about any recent revelations from God? Oh yes, he goes on once in a while

---

1. E.g., see 1 Cor 11:29. For an excellent discussion, cf. Wayne Grudem, *The Gift of Prophecy in 1 Corinthians* (Washington: University of America Press, 1982). He convincingly argues that in terms of authority status the New Testament analogy of the Old Testament prophet is an *apostle* (in the narrow sense).

about his Damascus road conversion, and how he saw the resurrected Lord; but everyone knows you can't build today's spiritual giant out of yesterday's spiritual experience. Has he known anything of real, spiritual vitality this past week? And if he has had any worthwhile visions, why hasn't he talked about them?

The truth of the matter is that Paul is most reluctant to talk about his visions and revelations. Luke tells us of a number of visions that Paul received (Acts 9:12; 16:9-10; 18:9-10; 22:17-21; 23:11; 27:23-24) so Paul must have talked about some of them with his closest colleagues. This is not altogether surprising in those instances where guidance was involved, as others would have to be given the rationale for Paul's plans, or where sharing the vision meant the apostle was admitting to his own deep discouragement or fear. What is remarkable, however, is that in his epistles Paul does not normally share the content of any vision or revelation (if there is a difference between the two terms, the latter has the larger range of meaning, the former being a revelation that involves apparent sight). In the text before us, Paul tells us at least one reason for his silence: he believes there is nothing to be gained by such talk, i.e., no spiritual profit for the Corinthians if he exposes his most intimate and super-natural spiritual experiences to them. Such talk may puff him up, or help to establish his reputation; but what *good* would it do? None, as far as the apostle can see; and so in the past he has held his peace.

Yet in this case, he is forced into it. Because he is driven by the fickle allegiance of the Corinthians and their spiritual danger, he reasons that more is to be lost by not boasting than by boasting; so once again he prepares to make a fool of himself (2 Cor 12:11). In this case, unlike most of the previous entries on the list (cf. chap. 5), he cannot simply boast about the opposite in a cutting parody. What, after all, is the opposite of receiving visions and revelations except not receiving them? To boast about not receiving them would in this instance be both untrue and dangerous: untrue, because Paul had indeed received spectacular revelations; and dangerous, because it would be playing right into his detractors' hands.

That is why Paul adopts a slightly different approach in these verses (12:1-10), an approach we shall unravel in the next few pages.

B. A Man in Christ—in the Third Person (12:2-4)!

"I know a man in Christ," Paul says, "who fourteen years ago was caught up to the third heaven" (2 Cor 12:2). It sounds at first as if Paul is talking about someone else, a Christian of his aquaintance who enjoyed a spectacular visionary experience almost a decade and a half previously. But it is soon clear that Paul is actually talking about himself. This is obvious not because Paul knows the time and content of the vision—after all, the "man in Christ" might have passed such information on to Paul—but for three other reasons. First, Paul is forced to admit in verse 6, however reluctantly, that if he were to boast of such a vision, he would not be a fool—i.e., his boasting would be grounded in fact. Second, Paul ties together the experience of this vision with his own reception of a thorn (v. 7). This would make no sense if the man in Christ is not to be identified with Paul: Why should Paul receive a debilitating thorn to be kept humble after another person has enjoyed the "surpassingly great revelations"? Third, for Paul to boast about another person's revelations when his detractors are out to demean the apostle himself, not some unknown third party, makes no contextual sense.

There can be no serious doubt, then, that Paul is referring to himself when he tells what happened to the man in Christ. The important question is why he uses this circumlocution. The answer can only be that he is so embarrassed to have to boast at all that the closest approximation he can manage to the conduct he finds so despicable is to write of himself in the third person. And even so, he writes not of a great apostle but of a man in Christ, so that when his readers discover a few verses later that Paul is really talking about himself, they will not place him in a super-Christian class, a cut above the common herd. Whatever revelations Paul received came to him, not as to an extraordinary apostle, but as to a Christian, a man in Christ. Not a trace of merit theology or lurking pride peeps through Paul's language.

This second canonical epistle to the Corinthians was apparently written about A.D. 55 or 56. Whether we reckon up the "fourteen years" inclusively or not, this puts the visionary experience into the silent decade of Paul's ministry, roughly A.D. 35-45, years about which we know almost nothing save that he spent them in Syria and Cilicia (Gal 1:21). Doubtless Paul was already discharging the responsibilities the Lord laid on him at his conversion—to carry the name of Jesus "before the Gentiles and their kings and before the people of Israel" and to suffer for that same name (Acts 9:15, 16). Probably much of the suffering and some at least of the beatings and floggings listed in 1 Corinthians 11 were inflicted during that period; and now we learn that the same period, unreported by Luke in the book of Acts, also brought Paul the most astounding revelation he ever received. Our knowledge of Paul and of the other apostles is very fragmentary; and were it not for these chapters of 2 Corinthians, it would be incomparably more so.

What, then, happened to Paul on this occasion? We may summarize what Paul tells us of it in three points:

1. Paul was caught up to "the third heaven," to "Paradise" (12:2,4). Jews of the period often spoke of a multiplicity of heavens (cf. Paul's "all the heavens" in Eph 4:10, rendered "the whole universe" by the NIV); but the exact number of them was not agreed. Some of the intertestamental sources speak of five, seven, ten, or some other number of heavens. Seven is perhaps the most common (e.g., *Testament of Levi* 2:7; *Assumption of Isaiah* 6:13; Babylonian Talmud *Hagigah* 12*b*); but it is unlikely Paul is saying he was caught up to the third heaven of seven, since the point of his account is the unexcelled blessedness of what he saw and heard. Paul must be using a three-heaven scheme in this passage; and if so, Calvin's view, that third heaven indicates here what is highest and best, is probably correct. Certainly many sources speak of three heavens, and some of them relate the third heaven to paradise (e.g., *2 Enoch* 8; *Apocalypse of Moses* 37:5).

The word "paradise" is a loan-word from Persian, in which it referred to the "park" a nobleman might own as part of his estate. Adopted by Greek-speaking Jews, it soon came to refer to the Garden of Eden, the first paradise. Because many Jews thought of the final state as a restoration, in some sense, of Eden, that final state of blessedness came to be called the last paradise (cf. Rev 2:7). Everything in between is the hidden paradise (cf. Luke 23:43). To identify paradise with the third heaven, therefore, is to make the third heaven the place of God's presence and the supreme goal for all who know him. Paul uses the language of his heritage to label the sphere to which he was caught up. The verb rendered "caught up" suggests a rapid transfer, not a slow ascent. How did this take place?

2. Paul is uncertain what state he was in during this revelation (12:2-3). Twice he speaks of his experience of being caught up to the third heaven in these or similar words: "Whether it was in the body or out of the body I do not know— God knows." To put it another way, Paul does not know whether he was caught up to the third heaven like an Enoch, body and all, or only in spirit, temporarily leaving his body behind. Clearly Paul does not think it matters too much. "Ignorance of the mode does not take away the certain knowledge of the thing" (Bengel). Possibly the false apostles focused a lot of attention on the details of their experiences, and less on their visionary substance. If so, Paul distances himself from his opponents in this respect as well.

Nevertheless Paul's repeated remark has been misunderstood in some recent commentaries and studies. It goes beyond the evidence, for instance, to argue that Paul could not imagine human life apart from either a natural body or a resurrection body, on the ground that he does not care to make the distinction between bodily existence and immaterial existence. Some reason this way because they do not believe the Bible teaches anything about an intermediate state. They hold that when a believer dies he immediately receives a resurrection body with no point of continuity with his dead natural body.

That interpretation misses the point in this passage. Paul says he does not *know* his state when he experiences the vision; but the fact that he can articulate the alternatives, "whether in the body or out of the body," shows he is perfectly comfortable with either, and can envisage either as an appropriate mode in which to enjoy his sojourn in paradise.

Of course, Paul did not write these words to settle such questions, but simply to express his own uncertainty as to the state he was in when he was caught up into the third heaven.

3. The revelations Paul received were beyond all normal spiritual experience (12:4). Paul heard "inexpressible things, things that man is not permitted to tell." Some see only one restriction in these words: i.e., the things Paul saw were inexpressible, not in the sense that these were ineffable, but in that Paul was forbidden to express them. In that case the next words, "things that man is not permitted to tell," add nothing new, but merely clarify the meaning of "inexpressible things." Parallels are often adduced from Philo or the mystery religions.

The parallels do not strike me as very convincing. For instance, in Apuleius (*Metamorphoses* 11.23), Lucius finds no difficulty articulating what he is forbidden to tell (on the grounds that his readers are pious and will themselves keep the secret!); so the alleged parallel is not very close. The easiest way to understand "inexpressible things" is take it to mean "ineffable." This means there are *two* restraints on Paul's communication of his vision: first, it was inexpressible or ineffable; and second, even if he wanted to disclose the ineffable (presumably by using many metaphors), he was in any case forbidden to do so.

Both restraints tell us important things. The first may be clarified by a parallel problem. Suppose you learned the language of some isolated tribe in the interior of New Guinea from a tribesman who made the trek out to the "civilized" world. The tribe, let us say, is pre-Stone Age in its technology; and your assignment is to penetrate that tribe and explain to the people, using their language and no visual aids, exactly what electricity is and can do.

You might proceed by saying that electricity (presumably you would have to transliterate the word) is something like a powerful, invisible spirit that runs faster than the wind along hard things like vines. These hard things, unlike vines, are made by men, and are often strung up on tree trunks with their branches lopped off. The electricity is made at one end of these "vines," and the vines carry the electricity into all the houses. When it gets inside, it goes into some other things that man makes. One of these looks a little like a box; but when electricity gets inside of it, the top heats up like fire, and the cooking can be done indoors and without smoke. When the electricity gets inside other things that man makes—small, round things—they fill the house with light, as if they were little suns.

So far, of course, you haven't ventured into batteries, motors, moving staircases, electric clocks, thermostats, refrigerators, pocket calculators, or computers; and already the assignment seems pretty formidable. The problem lies not with the native intelligence of the tribal folk, but with the limitations of their experience. They have few mental hooks on which to hang this new information, because they have not seen or experienced most of the things you wish to describe, or anything very much like them. That is why you have resorted to so many metaphors and similes: wires are something like vines that man makes, a stove is a bit like a box whose top gets hot when the electricity enters, and so forth.

How then shall we describe, as it were, the throne room of God? If a Paul is caught up into the third heaven and witnesses remarkable things, how could he possibly talk about them with any fluency except to those with similar experience? The same is true, of course, whenever prophet or apostle was permitted to see something of the glory of the LORD. If these privileged visionaries were permitted to talk about their experiences at all, they were invariably restricted to metaphorical language of some sort. Thus Ezekiel summarizes his inaugural vision this way: "This was the appearance of the likeness of the glory of the LORD. When I saw it, I fell facedown, and I heard the voice of the one speaking" (Ezek 1:28b). Something similar takes place in John's vision of the exalted Christ (Rev 1:12-17).

God's throne and glory, the paradise he is creating for his own, the new heaven and the new earth, all evoke imagination-stretching ideas by the use of symbols and metaphors; but our knowledge of them is fragmentary and often symbolic. If the new heaven and the new earth is "the home of righteousness" (2 Pet 3:13), we can begin to understand, by extrapolation, that everything that takes place there is just, honest, right, untainted by sin; but the full ramifications of even such a simple statement still leave us behind, even as they draw us onward.

What Paul saw in his vision was inexpressible. This does not mean that he underwent an experience so mystical he could not put it into words, still less that, although the experience involved objective features, it was the sort of thing that could not be talked about under any circumstances, but that the things Paul saw were inexpressible once the apostle returned to his normal sphere of service. No one around Paul had enjoyed similar revelations, so there was no bridge of common experience on this topic. The vision remained fundamentally "inexpressible."

At the same time, Paul tells us the things he heard are those "that man is not permitted to tell" (2 Cor 12:4). This does not make them superfluous or useless, but private: i.e., they were not given to Paul so that he would pass them on to the church, but solely for his own benefit. The New Testament often encourages Christians to live with eternity's values and prospects in view, recognizing that we are but pilgrims in transit down here. Most of us are largely shielded from the quantity and quality of the trials Paul faced; and we often do not live up to the light we have already received. But God's purpose for Paul involved the apostle in staggering sufferings, formidable opposition, and quite incredible challenges; and so to fortify him for his service and sufferings, the God of all hope displayed to the apostle a little more of the glory to come than most of us perceive, so that it would serve as an anchor for his soul in the roughest weather. Even the glimpses of glory the New Testament gives us have as their purpose the promotion of holiness, steadfastness, and faith, not the satisfaction of idle curiosity (e.g., 2 Pet 3:10-14; 1 John 3:2-3). Therefore it is not surprising if the spectacular revelations afforded the apostle to the Gentiles, this "man in Christ," were designed for his own special strengthening to help him persevere to the end undaunted—not to satisfy the curiosity of immature believers like the Corinthians who would use the material to bolster their pride, not to increase their faith. For this reason, the things Paul heard were both inexpressible (in that they could not be adequately presented to others with no personal experience of them) and secret. They were entirely beyond the normal spiritual experience of most believers.

Apart from this, Paul does not tell us what he experienced; for to do so would obviously have violated the restraints on communication God himself had imposed. Nevertheless, God in his mercy providentially brought Paul to tell us this much, so that even if our minds cannot fully explore this revelation's content, our imaginations may glimpse a small gleam of the surpassingly great glory that was shown Paul and will one day be ours. In that sense, we too in a small way share in the encouragement and upward call which these revelations provided for the apostle Paul.

C. The Response of an Apostle to Surpassingly Great Revelations (12:5-6a)

1. He still prefers to boast of his weakness (12:5-6a). The apostle now delicately reconciles the two Pauls, the man in Christ and Paul himself. He wants to emphasize the utterly exceptional nature of the revelations he has just mentioned, and therefore the amazing honor graciously afforded the person who received them; and so, maintaining the ruse of the third-person visionary a few words longer, he writes, "I will boast about a man like that" (2 Cor 12:5a). Under no circumstance, however, does Paul want to gain credit or reputation from these revelations, if any of his readers are beginning to see through Paul's literary device. To emphasize the magnitude of the honor given, he will boast about the "man in Christ"; but as far as his own fundamental commitments to proper boasting are concerned (presented in 10:12-18), he still must add, "but I will not boast about myself, except about my weaknesses" (v. 5b)

At this point his readers must be a trifle uncertain. Now Paul removes any vestige of the guise. "Even if I should choose to boast [as if I really were the man in Christ]" he writes, "I would not be a fool, because I would be speaking the truth" (12:6a), i.e., if he claimed these things for himself he would not be exposed as a lying fool because in fact he would be shown to be speaking the truth when he made the claim. There! At last Paul has done it: he has confessed himself to be the person who was afforded these surpassingly great revelations. He had little choice. But he has taken this step with extraordinary subtlety. He has again called himself a fool for entering into this boasting game, insisted that he received these visions as a common "man in Christ," distanced himself from this hypothetical "man in Christ," made the connection in hypothetical language ("Even if I should choose to boast. . . ."), and stressed again his profound commitment to boasting only of his weaknesses.

The depth of this commitment is remarkable. Paul was far from parading his deepest spiritual experiences; and the most profound of these he would have taken unmentioned to the grave had it not been for the peculiar circumstances that called forth this confession. He believed, not only in theory but in practice, the Scripture he preached to others: "Let him who boasts boast in the Lord" (2 Cor 10:17).

But why?

2. He fears that others will think too highly of him (12:6b).
Most of us spend our lives in fear that others will not think highly

enough of us; but Paul, offered the opportunity to boast straight-forwardly about the most spectacular revelation ever afforded him, writes, "But I refrain, so no one will think more of me than is warranted by what I do or say."

Three convictions clearly underlie this restraint. *First,* Paul refuses to let his reputation rest on inaccessible claims, appeals to ecstatic or supernatural visions. Even Paul's Damascus road experience and his subsequent meeting with Ananias had some reluctant witnesses; and therefore it is set apart from the very private vision mentioned here.

The *second* conviction is the complement of the first. Paul will permit only his open conduct, what he does and says, to be used by his converts as the basis of their assessment of him. Behavior is of unsurpassed importance in the Christian way. No matter how spectacular the private claim, no matter how esoteric the putative vision, it cannot displace conduct and speech as more reliable indicators of how closely anyone follows Christ.

But the *third* and most remarkable underlying attitude is that Paul is genuinely concerned lest others think too highly of him. This might simply reflect a brutal honesty: he knows his own heart well enough to realize that, apart from grace, it is capable of the most appalling abominations in God's eyes (cf. Rom 3:10-20). But in fact it is more: it is the typical attitude displayed by this apostle, who is always concerned to insist that people should focus on the gospel and on the Savior, not the messenger. He will be a more effective witness to the message of Christ crucified if he draws little attention to himself and to his grace-empowered victories, being all the while unafraid to endure suffering, priva-tion, and disgrace.

D. Surpassingly Great Revelations— and Satan's Messenger (12:7-10)

Paul has been responding to the super-spiritual visionaries, who were relying on the stories of their spiritual prowess and ecstatic experiences to bolster their authority while deprecating Paul. By using the device of a third person "man in Christ," Paul relates his own most astonishing revelation, while nevertheless distancing himself from the bragging characteristic of his oppo-nents. But there is another reason why Paul is prepared to relate the story: it is inextricably tied up with a further experience, the story of his thorn in the flesh. This second phase of Paul's spectacular revelatory experience not only says exactly what the apostle wants to say, but makes it impossible to believe that Paul is actually surreptitiously building his own reputation; for he of all people understands best that in the Christian way great grace and great privilege often go hand in hand with great suffering.

1. God and Satan—to keep Paul from conceit (12:7). A great deal of energy has been poured into identifying Paul's thorn in the flesh. Explanations are legion, and include malaria, a serious eye condition, feelings of guilt and depression owing to Paul's failure to convert his fellow Jews, Jewish persecution, epilepsy, a marked speech defect, some sort of continued temptation (taking "flesh" to refer to unregenerate nature), and many more. Several of the suggestions are plausible, none capable of proof. What seems clear, however, is that Paul's thorn in the flesh, whatever it was, came to him *after* his "surpassingly great revelations," and in consequence of them. In other words, it was not a birth defect or an impediment of character that had afflicted him long before the time he enjoyed being caught up to the third heaven.

It is equally clear that this thorn was something substantial, not some minor irritation. An apostle who could willingly put up with the sufferings and deprivations listed in 1 Corinthians 11 would not beseech the Lord so strenuously and repeatedly for the removal of some minor problem that could easily be borne. Paul's thorn was something very painful or extraordinarily embarrassing, and perhaps both.

More important yet, Paul sees this thorn as simultaneously the work of Satan and the work of God. The thorn is "an angel (i.e., messenger) of Satan," something sent by the archfiend to wound, limit, and defeat the apostle. Certainly Satan is capable of inflicting grievous physical damage (Job 2:1-10; 1 Cor 5:5; 1 Tim 1:20), in addition to his work of moral seduction, and sometimes the former is the complement or instrument of the latter. Since the thorn is Satan's messenger, we are not surprised to find Paul turning to God for its removal. Should not Christians expect God to remove Satan's obstacles? There may be special circumstances, like those of Job; but is not God normally interested in defeating Satan?

But the problem is more complex than that, for Paul also believes that this thorn came to him from God. He writes in the passive: "there was given me"—almost certainly an instance of the so-called divine passive, i.e., "there was given me by God." Lest there be any doubt, the purpose of this "gift" is to keep Paul from becoming conceited. Satan would certainly not be interested in that goal. His interests would be much better served if Paul were to become insufferably arrogant. The stated purpose of this gift must therefore be God's: although the thorn is a messenger from Satan, it was nonetheless simultaneously given to Paul by God himself, whose purpose in giving it was beneficent: to keep Paul from becoming conceited.

There is a general lesson of considerable importance here. Many people go through life trying to isolate this incident or that event as the exclusive work of Satan or the exclusive work of God. This almost always leads to doubtful interpretations of events, and may end up in a cultic view of guidance. Certainly this approach does not listen very carefully to what the Scriptures say on these matters.

Consider the death of Jesus Christ. Luke recognizes that the sequence of betrayal, arrest, torture, rigged courts, and crucifixion is the hour "when darkness reigns" (Luke 22:53); he explicitly states that all this came about "with the help of wicked men" (Acts 2:23) and as the result of an ugly conspiracy (4:27). Yet at the same time, all these events came about as a result of what God's "power and will had decided beforehand should happen" (v. 28). Thus there is a sense in which the death of Jesus was a work of great evil, and all responsible for it are culpable; but there is also a sense in which it was a work of God acting in love, the result of his redemptive purpose to establish a new humanity under a new covenant sealed with the blood of his Son. It is not that God came into the plan after the fact and turned it around for good. Far from it: the Bible insists it was God's plan from the beginning, the very reason why he sent his Son in the first place. Yet God's sovereignty in the matter does not in any way diminish the responsibility of all those connected with Jesus' death.

I have dealt with this theme at length elsewhere,[2] and do not wish to take it up again here. Nevertheless its implications are

2. D. A. Carson; *Divine Sovereignty and Human Responsibility* (Atlanta: John Knox, 1981).

substantial for the way Christians regard the tragedies of life. Some believers, very concerned to be spiritual, try to treat death, e.g., only as victory. It is a "homegoing," a "call to higher service," an "elevation to our higher calling." Does not Paul himself tell us that to be absent from the body is to be present with the Lord? If there are tears, surely they are tears of self-pity and shock among those left behind; but death itself is not ugly, and certainly it is nothing a mature Christian should fear or despise.

This approach to death is too one-sided. The Bible still treats death as an enemy, the "last enemy" that only the return of Christ will conquer (1 Cor 15:25-26). Death remains the stark proof of sin, the result of the curse, the evidence of the divine indictment under which the race stands; and it will not be finally defeated until the dawning of the new heaven and the new earth. Meanwhile, there is a sense in which we *ought* to "rage, rage against the dying of the light" (though not in the sense Dylan Thomas gave those words): death is the result of sin, and everything to do with the domain of sin we should detest.

What we must therefore do is preserve the balance of Scripture. Death is an enemy; but it is an enemy principially defeated by Christ's cross-work and slated for final destruction when he returns. Death is the unflagging seal of the curse, of our racial and personal condemnation; but it is also the means God used in Christ to purchase our redemption: the Son died, the just for the unjust, to bring us to God. Death is *not* intrinsically good, for it speaks eloquently of sin, curse, corruption, mortality; but God's grace already abounds so mightily that believers know death is not the ultimate reality. We may grieve, but not as those with no hope: departure to be with Christ is far better.

This same balance ought to inform our perspectives on many areas of life still stamped by the curse. Disease, accidents, oppression, opposition to the gospel: none of these is a good thing, and all of them can be traced in one way or another to Satan himself. None of these will find any place in the consummated kingdom. Yet at the same time, none of these ugly things escapes the outermost bounds of God's sovereignty. "We know that in *all* things God works for the good of those who love him, who have been called according to his purpose" (Rom 8:28).

Paul knows these truths well, and he reflects them in this most difficult test in his life. "To keep me from becoming conceited because of the surpassingly great revelations," he writes, "there was given me a thorn in my flesh, a messenger of Satan, to torment me" (2 Cor 12:7—this is the translation of the most likely textual variant). The thorn was a messenger of Satan—there was nothing intrinsically good about it, and no amount of pious talk could ever cover up the fact. Nevertheless, it was "given" him (by God) for beneficent purposes.

Perhaps Paul remembered a similar situation in the Old Testament. The eleven brothers sold Joseph into slavery, a base, evil action; but reflecting on it years later, Joseph himself could say to his brothers, "You intended to harm me, but God intended it for good to accomplish what is now being done, the saving of many lives" (Gen 50:20). So in Paul's case: the immediate *reason* for the thorn, from God's point of view, was the surpassingly great revelations; and its immediate *purpose* was to keep Paul from becoming conceited.

It is no small credit to the apostle that he recognized this purpose. Just as others might be encouraged to think too highly of Paul if they found out about these great revelations, so Paul might find himself in the same danger. "How dangerous must self-exaltation be, when even the apostle required so much restraint" (Fausset). Paul understands this so well that in 2 Corinthians 12:7-10, where he discusses his experience with the thorn in the flesh, there is no longer even a hint of his earlier man-in-Christ circumlocution. About his greatest revelations, he speaks only with circumspection, if at all; about his weaknesses, he speaks directly and without bashfulness. In short, even by retelling this painful experience, he is exemplifying the lessons he learned by it, and which he articulates in the remaining verses (8-10).

2. Paul's plea and God's grace (12:8-9a).

Nothing that I have said suggests Paul enjoyed the thorn. Whether it was perceived as a messenger from Satan or a burden pressed on him by the Father, Paul felt it was too much to be borne. "Three times I pleaded with the Lord to take it away from me," Paul writes. Clearly these were not casual prayers, carelessly offered at the spur of the moment, but three separate and sustained periods of intercession directed to Jesus himself.[3]

3. Normally in Paul the articular *ho Kyrios* refers to the Lord Jesus, whereas the anarthrous form *Kyrios* refers to Yahweh. It is more usual to

God's answer was not, at first, what Paul wanted to hear. Nevertheless it was God's standing answer (the Greek should be rendered, "But he has said to me. . . ."). The answer itself is often repeated in hymn and song, but must not have been easy to accept when first given: "My grace is sufficient for you, for my power is made perfect in weakness" (2 Cor 12:9a).

In one sense, of course, God did indeed answer Paul's prayer; but not as the apostle wished. Calvin rightly distinguishes between means and ends in prayer. The end that Paul wanted was relief from the thorn, and he simply assumed that the means would be the thorn's removal. But God granted the ends by another means: he gave relief from the thorn, not by removing it, but by adding more grace, sufficient grace. The Lord promised Paul that in the distress caused by this messenger from Satan, he would always find that divine grace afforded him a sufficient supply to enable him to bear up as a Christian.

Moreover, this divine grace bestowed on Paul was sufficient precisely because Paul was so weak. God's strength is made perfect in weakness: it reaches its fullest measure and most powerful forms when issued in response to weakness. The greater the Christian's weakness, the greater the grace poured out.

If this is true, then the self-proclaimed strengths of the false apostles mean they are devoid of grace! All the impressive credentials of these ecclesiastics turn out to signify bankruptcy in grace. Grace responds to need, acknowledged weakness, spiritual destitution. The kingdom of heaven goes to the poor in spirit (Matt 5:3).

It is important to recognize what this wonderful text does *not* promise. Some read it as if the believer may go through a period of weakness followed by a period of divine grace and strength, where the Christian becomes a kind of conqueror. The weakness becomes a condition of this strength, a payment of dues if you like. But such an interpretation twists the text. Paul's thorn is not followed by grace; rather, grace is given him to enable him to cope with the weakness that is not removed. Very often in the Scripture, weakness is not the condition of grace in the sense that it serves as the necessary precursor of grace, but in the sense that

pray to the Father, or (to use the entire formula) to pray to the Father through Christ and in the Holy Spirit; but there are several prayers in the New Testament addressed directly to Christ (e.g., here; Acts 7:59).

it serves as a continuing vehicle of grace. "It is when he is weak, really weak—poor, sick, humiliated, despised, unloved by his own spiritual children as well as scorned by the world—that God's power comes into view. For 'God's foolishness is wiser than men, and God's weakness is stronger than men' (I Cor.i.25)" (Barrett).

Nowhere is this clearer than in Romans 8, the famous more-than-conquerors passage. Paul is not interested in establishing a breed of super-triumphalists for whom every enterprise is success-ful, every mission fruitful, every endeavor prosperous. Far from it. He demonstrates that Christians are more than conquerors in the context of trouble, hardship, persecution, famine, nakedness, and sword, and in the sense that despite all these things God's love will sustain us, maintain us, and buoy us up in faithfulness so that we shall never be separated from the love of God that is in Christ Jesus our Lord (vv. 31-39).

This was also the pattern supremely manifest by Christ Jesus our Lord. The cross itself, that fearful, Roman sign of ignominy, defeat, judgment, and death was precisely the means by which Jesus triumphed over all his foes. God's strength was supremely manifest in Jesus' weakness. Why then should Jesus' disciples choose to disparage his example by siding with triumphalists? Kierkegaard was not wrong to pray:

> O Lord Jesus Christ, many and various are the things to which a man may feel himself drawn, but one thing there is to which no man ever felt himself drawn in any way, that is, to suffering and humiliation. This we men think we ought to shun as far as possible, and in any case that we must be compelled to it. But Thou, our Saviour and Redeemer, Thou who wast humbled yet without compulsion, and least of all compelled to that humiliation in the imitation of which man discovers his highest honor; ah, that the picture of Thee in Thy humiliation might be so vivid to us that we might feel ourselves drawn unto Thee in lowliness, unto Thee who from on high wilt draw all unto Thyself.[4]

3. Paul's response and articulated principle (12:9b-10). Paul learns the lesson. After three serious sessions of prayer, he comes to grips with the wisdom of the Lord's response; and so far from begrudgingly acceding to what he cannot change, he writes:

---

4. Soren Kierkegaard.

"Therefore I will boast all the more gladly about my weaknesses, so that Christ's power may rest on me. That is why, for Christ's sake, I delight in weaknesses, in insults, in hardships, in persecutions, in difficulties. For when I am weak, then I am strong." Paul could well have written the lines:

> The glorious revelations you've bestowed,
> Ineffable displays of holy light,
> Call forth my joyful praise in sheer delight,
> A foretaste of my heavenly abode.
> Then why this ceaseless thorn, this painful goad
> Of Satan? Why not spare me from the blight
> Of persecution, malice, danger's fright?
> From what strange streams of love have nettles flowed?
>   Sufficient is my grace for you: indeed,
>   My power is perfected when you're weak.
>   Will you for your own feeble prowess plead,
>   When bankrupt weakness brings the strength you seek?
> Now insults, hardships, weakness are my song,
> My joy; for when I'm weak, then I am strong.[5]

In short, Paul is not some foolhardy masochist who likes to get hurt, who loves to be abused. Instead, we find him a rational and devout Christian whose experience with the thorn in the flesh brought him to a carefully weighed perspective about boasting, a perspective that has sustained all he has written in these chapters. He will gladly boast about his weaknesses if it means Christ's power will rest on him. "To be made thus the dwelling-place of the power of Christ, when he reveals his glory, was a rational ground of rejoicing in those infirmities which were the condition of his presence and the occasion of the manifestation of his power" (Hodge).

Lest the Corinthians, largely seduced by the triumphalists, have still missed Paul's point, he repeats his decision (12:9b) as an articulated personal principle (12:10). Paul is prepared to stop praying for the removal of the thorn, not because he enjoys this or any other messenger of Satan, but because he knows that the "power of Christ manifests to the full its irresistible energy and attains its highest results by performing works of power with

5. D. A. Carson, *Sonnets from Scripture.*

powerless instruments" (Wilson). That is why Paul is prepared to extend the lesson learned from one particular thorn in the flesh to include weaknesses, hardships, persecutions, and difficulties. Wherever he is weak, there also does God's power enjoy the greatest opportunity to manifest itself with full vigor.

Everything depends on the phrase "for Christ's sake"; for as Tasker comments, "Only a morbid fanatic can take pleasure in the sufferings he inflicts upon himself; only an insensitive fool can take pleasure in the sufferings that are consequences of his own folly; and only a convinced Christian can take pleasure in sufferings endured *for Christ's sake*, for he alone has been initiated into the divine secret, that it is only when he is weak . . . that he is strong." The super-spiritual visionaries who have afflicted the church know nothing of such Christianity. Paul's response, his boasting in weakness, would be nearly meaningless to them. But men and women who know and love Jesus will readily discern why Paul reaches these revolutionizing conclusions, for they have begun to grasp what it means to serve and suffer "for Christ's sake" (12:10). And as they serve, they can trust his perfect combination of sovereignty and grace, enabling them to sing:

> A sovereign protector I have,
>   Unseen, yet forever at hand,
> Unchangeably faithful to save,
>   Almighty to rule and command.
> He smiles, and my comforts abound;
>   His grace as the dew shall descend,
> And walls of salvation surround
>   The soul He delights to defend.
>
> Inspirer and hearer of prayer,
>   Thou shepherd and guardian of Thine,
> My all to Thy covenant care
>   I sleeping and waking resign.
> If Thou art my shield and my sun,
>   The night is no darkness to me;
> And, fast as my moments roll on,
>   They bring me but nearer to Thee.
>
>   Augustus Montague Toplady (1740-78)

7

Open Rebuke:
The Failures of the Corinthians and the Motives of the Apostle

2 Corinthians 12:11-21

[11] I have made a fool of myself, but you drove me to it. I ought to have been commended by you, for I am not in the least inferior to the "super-apostles," even though I am nothing. [12] The things that mark an apostle—signs, wonders and miracles—were done among you with great perseverance. [13] How were you inferior to the other churches, except that I was never a burden to you? Forgive me this wrong!

[14] Now I am ready to visit you for the third time, and I will not be a burden to you, because what I want is not your possessions but you. After all, children should not have to save up for their parents, but parents for their children. [15] So I will very gladly spend for you everything I have and expend myself as well. If I love you more, will you love me less? [16] Be that as it may, I have not been a burden to you. Yet, crafty fellow that I am, I caught you by trickery! [17] Did I exploit you through any of the men I sent you? [18] I urged Titus to go to you and I sent our brother with him. Titus did not exploit you, did he? Did we not act in the same spirit and follow the same course?

[19] Have you been thinking all along that we have

been defending ourselves to you? We have been
speaking in the sight of God as those in Christ; and
everything we do, dear friends, is for your strengthening. [20] For I am afraid that when I come I may
not find you as I want you to be, and you may not
find me as you want me to be. I fear that there may
be quarreling, jealousy, outbursts of anger, factions,
slander, gossip, arrogance and disorder. [21] I am
afraid that when I come again my God will humble
me before you, and I will be grieved over many
who have sinned earlier and have not repented of
the impurity, sexual sin and debauchery in which
they have indulged.

There is a time for subtle dealings: there is
also a time for blunt confrontation. As a wise counselor, Paul
knows the difference. He has built a very strong case against the
intruding apostles, and exposed the fundamentally unChristian
structure of their triumphalism. But so far Paul has been
relatively gentle with the Corinthians themselves. He has shamed
them a little with his irony, and demanded that they think
through the criteria of Christian leadership they have been fed
by the interlopers; but he has not launched an open assault on
their own complicity in the troubling state of affairs the false
apostles have introduced into the Corinthian church.

In the verses before us, that changes. Paul details some of the
specific failures of the Corinthians in this sorry affair; and then,
lest his reasons for bringing them up be impugned yet again, he
reveals some of his own deep motives for doing so. We may
profitably learn to avoid the failures of the one and to nurture
the motives of the other.

A. The Failures of the Corinthians (12:11-18)

*1. The Corinthians have driven Paul to the agony of these
chapters (12:11).* Paul's foolish boasting is now pretty well over.
Boasting was certainly not something the apostle wanted to do.
After all, he had condemned the habits of others in this regard,
and insisted that the biblical pattern was to boast only in the
Lord (2 Cor 10:7-18). Nevertheless, Paul was driven to indulge in

what he condemned. Of course, most of what he did was cast in terms of deep and sometimes scathing irony; and the entire series of boasts, he insisted, was in any case not the mark of Paul the Christian, but Paul the fool (11:17). If at some point he actually did claim something for himself such as the fact that he had been the recipient of surpassingly great revelations, he did so with the lightest touch, indeed through an embarrassing and awkward appeal to a third-person "man in Christ." And even then Paul turned immediately from what might have become real boasting to boasting about his weaknesses.

The entire procedure has been eminently detestable to Paul. It may have been necessary in order to save the church from spiritual charlatans and their false doctrine; but it was a personal agony for the apostle, as he indicates by saying yet again, "I have made a fool of myself."

In one sense, of course, the people responsible for bringing the apostle to this sorry state were the interlopers themselves. But there is another way of looking at the matter. If the Corinthians had been half as wise and discerning as they thought they were, they would not have been taken in by the "deceitful workmen" (2 Cor 11:13). "I have made a fool of myself," Paul admits; "but you drove me to it" (12:11). The pagan boasting of false leaders would never have forced Paul to adopt somewhat similar tactics, or a parody of them; only the silence of his own churches could do that, as his converts held their peace and were gradually taken in by the false apostles. Paul may have been forced to play the fool, but at least his action was excusable. Those who had driven Paul into this role could offer no excuse in their own defense.

No church was in a better position to defend and commend Paul than the one in Corinth. "I ought to have been commended by you," Paul goes on to say, "for I am not in the least inferior to the 'super-apostles,' even though I am nothing" (2 Cor 12:11b). This church was founded by Paul (1 Cor 4:14-16) and received all its early training in the way of righteousness from him; but when he is subtly maligned by these latecomer super-apostles, the Corinthians themselves, far from stoutly defending Paul and smartly turfing the interlopers out, have kept their peace about Paul and become the dupes of the frauds they should have disciplined.

Paul is not contradicting himself, begging for the kind of

letters of commendation his rivals made so much of (cf. 2 Cor
3:1). He well knew his apostleship was independent of men: its
origin was the commission he received from the Lord Jesus
himself (Gal 1:1); and no commendation could either add to or
take away from the authority and responsibility conferred on
him by that commission. Yet the Corinthians were his converts.
In that sense they were the seal or confirming sign of his
apostleship (1 Cor 9:2). Converted under Paul's apostolic ministry
(1 Cor 3:6,10; 4:15), they merely had to acknowledge that fact,
and they would have been commending his ministry. Pathetically, they failed to display even this minimum sign of gratitude. Preferring the worldly standards of leadership paraded
by the interlopers, the Corinthians began to feel ashamed that
their father in Christ was meek (10:1), short on rhetorical
flourishes v. 10; 11:6), not very secure financially (vv. 7-11; 12:13),
and reticent about his spiritual experiences (12:1-10).

The Corinthians should have seen instantly that Paul was "not
in the least inferior to the 'super-apostles'" in anything that was
truly a Christian value; and in other matters, the Corinthians had
to learn their criteria were wrong (see on 2 Cor 12:12-14, below).
Even this slight brush with boasting is enough to embarrass the
apostle, however; and so he quickly adds, "even though I am
nothing." Even his equivalence in every legitimate apostolic claim
has nothing to do with personal superiority: he is a debtor to
grace, and for Paul that is no mere cliché.

The Corinthian believers cannot be lumped together with the
interlopers; but they stand indicted in their own right. Their
failure to defend and commend Paul has been the immediate
cause of the spiritual agony he undergoes in composing these
chapters. Their sin was silence; yet it was not only silence, since:

2. The Corinthians utilized false criteria in assessing leaders (12:12-14). There are at least three of these. *First,* the Corinthians
succumbed to love of power and supernatural displays, forget-
ting that Paul's ministry was characterized by a distinctively
Christian balance of miracle and perseverance. In a syntactically
difficult verse, Paul says, "The things that mark an apostle—
signs, wonders and miracles—were done among you with great
perseverance." The last phrase could be rendered several differ-

ent ways. It seems unlikely, however, that it modifies the verb "were done," as if the apostle had perservered in his miracle-working at Corinth: i.e., in spite of opposition to miracles or personal fatigue. This does not easily square with what we know of Paul, nor fit the context before us very well.

It seems better to take the phrase to mean "in all endurance" (a more literal rendering of the Greek), in the sense "in (the context of) all endurance," so that the verse as a whole reads, "The things that mark an apostle—signs, wonders and miracles— were done among you in the context of all endurance." In other words, it sounds as if the Corinthians have been saying that if Paul really loved them he would have displayed more apostolic power. Perhaps the intruders were willing and able to parade their miracles. The Corinthians might ask, then, if Paul thought they were unworthy to receive his miracles. The apostle's reply is to this effect: No, you too witnessed many miracles typical of apostolic ministry, but they appeared in the context of great endurance. They were not triumphalistic bits of showmanship, but displays of the power of God revealed, as in the ministry of Jesus, in the midst of suffering and perseverance. The "endurance" in Paul's case would then refer to all the things mentioned in 2 Corinthians 11 and 12, including the beatings, the privations, and the thorn in the flesh.

This interpretation therefore suits the preceding, but it also fits with what comes next: Paul asks, "How were you inferior . . . ?" In other words, the Corinthians had apparently been feeling inferior, owing to Paul's treatment of them. They wanted miracles without suffering, triumphs without endurance; and their embittered memories were suggesting Paul had never really displayed his apostolic stuff to them at all! Paul's reply, then, is that "signs" (miracles with a peculiar ability to point beyond themselves and instruct the observer), "wonders" (miracles conceived as supernatural events that evoke awe) and "miracles" (lit., "mighty deeds," i.e., mighty displays of divine power that transcend what is normally seen in the course of nature) were indeed done among them: the Corinthians have no ground for complaint. But Paul refuses to say that *he* did the miracles: the passive "were done" is a nice touch, for Paul means the miracles "were done [*sc.* by God!]." He thereby avoids saying he himself performed them. As usual, Paul prefers not to cast his language as claim or boast. Moreover, he then adds that the miracles done were accomplished *in the context of great endurance.*

Although miracles in the post-Pentecost period of the New Testament are sometimes done by the hands of non-apostolic figures, normally apostles are the agents. In that sense, miracles constitute one "mark" of an apostle. But there are others, not least the stamina, endurance, and fortitude bound up in the phrase rendered "with great perseverance." The fault of the Corinthians was that their criteria for what is truly apostolic were painfully selective. They magnified the miracles and sapped all significance from suffering. They became true triumphalists; and their descendants are still with us.

The *second* false criterion espoused by the Corinthian believers is shown up by Paul's next sentence, a rhetorical question: "How were you inferior to the other churches, except that I was never a burden to you?" Then he adds, with cutting irony, "Forgive me this wrong!" (2 Cor 12:13). In part, this verse carries on from the last one. The Corinthians were not inferior in the number or kind of apostolic miracles performed among them; in fact, with but one exception, the Corinthians were not in any way treated as if they were an inferior breed. The one exception is that Paul refused to take money from the Corinthians. If that refusal made the Corinthians inferior, it is hard to see how— unless it made them feel inferior because their understanding of triumphalistic leadership inevitably cried out for strong authority figures who actually exploited them (11:7-12; 12:20-21)!

We have already learned something of Paul's reasoning on these matters. It was his normal fiscal practice to refuse help from the people to whom he was currently ministering. He might well accept it later, when it would help sustain him and his ministry in another mission field; but even then he was apparently reluctant to receive anything from any group in which triumphalism prevailed.

One way to get at the problem is to distinguish apostolic *marks* or *qualifications* from apostolic *rights*. Paul has the right of an apostle to be supported by the church or churches among which he is currently ministering; but he prefers not to use it (cf. 1 Cor 9:1-18; 2 Cor 11:5-12). That is one of the things that distinguishes a mark from a right. A mark or characteristic must be present in some sense; but a right need not be, since it might be cheerfully abandoned for some purpose of strategy, generosity, goodness. The Corinthians' error lay in transforming an apostolic right that Paul chose to forego into a necessary mark or qualification of apostolic office. Their error was a particular form of majoring in the minors.

In the *third* place, not only did the Corinthians fail to distinguish between apostolic mark and apostolic right, but they misinterpreted Paul's motives for not passing the hat among them. "Now I am ready to visit you for the third time" (on the numbering, cf. 2 Cor 13:1), Paul writes; and then he publicly resolves, "I will not be a burden to you, because what I want is not your possessions but you. After all, children should not have to save up for their parents, but parents for their children" (12:14). This third trip will not find Paul changing his financial policy; so the Corinthians had better get used to it. Indeed it is this very policy, a policy the Corinthians think strange and demeaning, that Paul uses to prove he is unlike the false apostles in his motives. Strange as his policy may be from the perspective of pagan one-upmanship, it forcefully demonstrates that what the apostle wants is not their possessions but them—i.e., he wants their continued allegiance and devotion to Christ, and their reciprocated love (6:13; 12:15). Far from making the Corinthians inferior, Paul's fiscal policy toward the Corinthians wisely exposes the exploiters for what they are, and presents a Christian value system to displace criteria based on money and power.

The illustration Paul adds ("After all, children should not have to save up for their parents, but parents for their children," 12:14b) should not be universalized. More extensive family responsibilities are set out in 1 Tim 5:8, responsibilities that presuppose a child may very well provide for an aging or infirm parent. Besides, Paul elsewhere defends the right of other apostles to be supported by their "children" (1 Cor 9:3-14). The point of Paul's illustration is, not that no other possible relationship may exist between parents and children, but that his motive toward the Corinthians is akin to that of a parent much concerned to bring his offspring to maturity and independence, not to exploit them.

The Corinthians, then, have driven Paul to the agony of these chapters and utilized false criteria in assessing leaders. The apostle now itemizes a third and a fourth failure on their part.

3. *The Corinthians have withheld their love from the apostle who has loved them so deeply (12:15-16a).* Paul has just said he acted toward the Corinthians as parents toward their children. He continues this theme, but utilizes it in a new way by emphasizing once more the depth of his commitment to them: "So I will very gladly spend for you everything I have and expend myself as well" (2 Cor 12:15a): he will cheerfully pour out on his converts not only whatever possessions he may have but his reserves of time and energy as well, so great is his love for them and his commitment to their maturity. But now the argument turns to point out this third Corinthian failure: "If I love you more, will you love me less?" (v. 15b). The comparatives "more" and "less" continue the analogy from verse 14. Paul is asking in effect, "If I love you more than parents love their children, will you love me less than children love their parents?"

One of the great Christian virtues is gratitude. Our first responsiblity in this area is to be grateful to God, not only for life itself, with all the blessings of common grace, but above all for forgiveness of our sins through Christ's voluntary self-sacrifice, and for all the benefits that have flowed to us on account of the Lord Jesus. It is generally true, however, that those who are grateful to God will also display a grateful attitude to others, not least to God's choice servants from whom they have derived so much good. Conversely, if Christians are singularly ungrateful to the older believers who have led them in their first steps of faith and discipleship, the failure probably reflects the kind of egocentric immaturity that is thankless toward God himself.

Christians bent on maturity should work hard at gratitude. Thankfulness to friends, parents, senior believers who have helped us on our way, and above all to God himself, is not only common courtesy, it is something more, much more: it is simultaneously a powerful antidote to bitterness and malice, and potent acknowledgment that we stand by grace. What else could ever displace gratitude as the appropriate response to grace, whether the special grace that brings us salvation or the grace mediated through fellow believers, friends, and events? Grace gives; what more can we do than give thanks? What response to grace could be more vile than ingratitude?

In an important sense, even our love finds its birth in gratitude: "This is how we know what love is: Jesus Christ laid down his life for us. . . . We love because he first loved us" (1 John 3:16; 4:19). All of our love for him is at best a response to his love for us. Conversely, failure to love him is a denial of his love for us. As such, it is a crude form of blasphemy, a slur on the love and grace of God manifest in Christ Jesus. By extension, the same vices are present in those who fail to reciprocate love to God's children.

The Corinthians out of simple thankfulness should have opened wide their hearts to the apostle and returned at least some portion of the love he had lavished on them. But supposing they remain stingy in their love, what will Paul's response be? Should he forego his fiscal policy and adopt the standards of the Corinthians? No, Paul could not do that; for in the current atmosphere, that would be akin to shifting from a theology of grace to a theology merit. The gospel itself would be eviscerated. Therefore Paul contemplates the past silence of the Corinthian believers, and recalls his own unswerving policy: "Be that as it may, I have not been a burden to you" (2 Cor 12:16a).

4. The Corinthians have suggested that Paul is financially corrupt (12:16b-18). Despite the fact that Paul has not taken any financial help from the Corinthian church (perhaps indeed because of it!), these believers have come to entertain the suggestion that Paul's fiscal independence was a cunning front that masked his financial corruption. He is charged with being unscrupulous and crafty by nature, traits used to enable him to extract money by guile from the Corinthians when he wouldn't take it openly and honestly. It is to this charge that Paul refers when he writes his next sentence with biting irony: "Yet, crafty fellow that I am, I caught you by trickery!"

It appears likely that the charge of financial fraud arose in connection with Paul's persistent appeals to the Corinthians for funds for the believers in depressed Jerusalem (1 Cor 16:1-4; 2 Cor 8-9). Probably someone started the rumor that Paul was going to use this money, or a substantial part of it, to line his own pockets. His assistants, they would say, come and pick up what we set aside and carry it to Paul; and who knows what happens to it then (wink, wink)? "It was not the smallest part of the hurtfulness of this charge that it touched Paul's assistants as well as himself" (Barrett).

Paul seeks to defend himself against this outrageous accusation by pointing out that the assistants he sent did not act like rapacious exploiters and bullies (unlike the false apostles!), but conducted themselves with the same spirit displayed by Paul. "Did I exploit you through any of the men I sent you?" Paul asks (2 Cor 12:17). In fact, the grammar of this rhetorical question is broken, probably owing to the intensity of emotion as Paul composes his letter: "Any of those I have sent—did I exploit you through him?" More explicitly, Paul continues, "I urged Titus to go to you and sent our brother with him. Titus did not exploit you, did he? Did we not act in the same spirit and follow the same course?" (12:18).[1] If the messengers Paul sent were not exploiters, why should the Corinthians think Paul himself was?

Probably the only thing that could finally allay all suspicion would be an appropriate letter of thanks from the Jerusalem church, a letter that would serve as a receipt. When Paul wrote these chapters the money had not yet been completely collected, let alone sent on; and therefore Paul's options for defending himself were extremely limited. The thrust of his reply is to shame the Corinthians into recognizing that the demeanor, self-denial, discipline, and integrity of Paul and his assistants are so demonstrable and obvious at every level of their dealings that the charges are absurd.

It is a reflection of the Corinthians' immaturity, of their sins before God, and of their brutal treatment of the apostle on so many fronts, that they have sunk so low. Sometimes, of course, our spiritual leaders do get sucked into dishonest or disreputable practices; and then they are to be rebuked publicly (1 Tim 5:20).

1. The movements of Titus have a bearing on the question of how 2 Corinthians was composed. If the trip of Titus and "our brother" (12:18) is the same as the trip promised in 8:16-24, a passage that anticipates the mission to Corinth of Titus along with "the brother who is praised by all the churches for his service to the gospel" (8:18) and "our brother who has often proved to us in many ways that he is zealous" (8:22), then 2 Cor 10-13 must have been written some time later than 2 Cor 1-9, since by 2 Cor 12:18 the trip has taken place, whereas in 2 Cor 8:16-24 it is still in the future. Alternatively, the trip Paul mentions in 12:18 may refer to an earlier journey of Titus to Corinth, alluded to in 8:6. On that journey Titus "made a beginning" toward the collection for the impoverished Christians in Jerusalem. In that case 2 Cor 10-13 would not have to be cut off so decisively from 2 Cor 1-9—although some have used the same identification to open up the possibility that 2 Cor 10-13 is to be identified with the "severe letter" written *before* 2 Cor 1-9. For discussion of the broader issues, see chap. 1 of this book.

But more often their public life and ministry leave them open to unfounded charges, and for that reason Christians are to be very slow even to listen to accusations against them. That the Corinthians could entertain such blatant nonsense about the apostle Paul is an index of their own attitudes and suspicions, their belief that money is important and all men want it, their lovelessness and ingratitude toward both God and Paul.

These failures in the Corinthians constitute the reason why the apostle must turn from this subject to a further elucidation of his own motives. If the Corinthians can actually believe Paul is characterized by graft and duplicity, they have not understood very well just what drives him. Thus the next paragraph, outlining some of Paul's motives, is part and parcel of the broader rebuke.

B. The Motives of the Apostle (12:19-21)

1. To strengthen the Corinthians (12:19). Paul is painfully aware that the Corinthians, judging by their past performance, might well display a remarkable ability to misunderstand and distort all that he is writing, and especially to twist his motives. With a little perverse encouragement, they might dismiss these admonitions as yet another sample of Paul's forceful writing style, a desperate strategy to scramble back into the good graces of the Corinthian church by pathetic self-defense.

The first sentence of verse 19 may be a question (as in NIV), or it may be a blunt statement: "You have been thinking all along that we have been defending ourselves to you." Either way, Paul denies the validity of their mental reservations, and details his true motives: "We have been speaking in the sight of God as those in Christ; and everything we do, dear friends, is for your strengthing" (2 Cor 12:19b).

Paul is so greatly aware that everything he says and does "is uncovered and laid bare before the eyes of him to whom we must give account" (Heb 4:13) that he could not possibly be involved in a petty power scramble. He has been speaking in the sight of God to whom ultimately he is accountable; he has been speaking as a Christian, as one of those in Christ. This theme dominates large parts of the Corinthian correspondence, probably because the Corinithians are so irresponsible in their use of language, in their boasting, in their personal relationships that they expect all others to partake in the same irresponsibility. It is said that one of the greatest punishments of the liar is not that he is not believed but that he will not believe. Similarly, the person who is undisciplined in his speech and selfish in his motives may face his greatest danger not in being rejected by others but in foolishly rejecting wise and disciplined and unselfish Christians. Paul does not fit their mold; and so he must explain to them, again and again, "Unlike so many, we do not peddle the word of God for profit. On the contrary, in Christ we speak before God with sincerity, like men sent from God" (2 Cor 2:17); or again, "Since, then, we know what it is to fear the Lord, we try to persuade men. What we are is plain to God, and I hope it is also to your conscience" (5:11); or again, as here, "We have been speaking in the sight of God as those in Christ."

In one sense, of course, Paul has indeed been defending himself. That is surely demonstrated by the fact that he has been forced by the Corinthians to engage in the foolish boasting. But when Paul in this verse denies that he is defending himself, he means only that he is not launching a defense of himself as the Corinthians measure self-defense. In the view of the Corinthian church, such self-defense is self-serving, and designed to promote self-interest and personal authority. If Paul were defending himself in that sense, it would mean the Corinthians are the judges who must assess what sort of man Paul is. But whatever Paul is doing here, he is not (he tells the Corinthians) defending himself "to you." He is so concerned to maintain God's approval (1 Cor 4:3-5) that he shows little interest in sinking to the judgment of lower courts.

With that perspective controlling Paul's outlook, then, his description of his motives cannot reasonably be challenged: "everything we do, dear friends, is for your strengthening" (2 Cor 12:19). The Corinthians have suspected Paul is writing to vindicate himself before them, whereas the truth is that he is writing to strengthen them, to build them up. If he could achieve this aim without winning them over in personal allegiance to himself that would not bother him in the slightest. Although the very nature of the contest makes such an option impossible, Paul's motives remain comfortably distanced from self-interest.

There is the mark of true Christian leadership. Sadly, too many leaders consciously or unconsciously link their own careers and reputations with the gospel they proclaim and the people they serve. Slowly, unnoticed by all but the most discerning, defense of the truth slips into self-defense, and the best interest of the congregation becomes identified with the best interest of the leaders. Personal triumphalism strikes again, sometimes with vicious intensity. It is found in the evangelical academic who invests all his opinions with the authority of Scripture, in the pastor whose every word is above contradiction, in the leader transparently more interested in self-promotion and the esteem of the crowd than in the benefit and progress of the Christians allegedly being served. It issues in political maneuvering, temper tantrums, a secular set of values (though never acknowledged as such), a smug and self-serving shepherd and hungry sheep.

We have much to learn from Paul. When in our hearts (and not merely in our verbal piety) our aim before God is to strengthen other believers, not to defend ourselves, we will not only succeed in revitalizing the church by our sacrificial ministry and example, but we shall also strike a powerful blow against the demonic heart of triumphalism, which is self in another guise. And if, with Paul, we sometimes face believers who completely misunderstand our motives, then at least we may be confident, with the apostle, that we have been speaking in the sight of God as those in Christ, and that the attacks may reveal more about the attackers than anything else. May God raise up many Christian leaders whose passion is to build up the body of Christ.

2. To promote candor and righteousness (12:20a). "For I am afraid that when I come I may not find you as I want you to be, and you may not find me as you want me to be" (2 Cor 12:20a). What the Corinthians would want out of a visit by Paul is not entirely certain, but presumably they would not want him to administer the whip (cf. 1 Cor 4:21), and they would like him not to upset their pagan perspectives. Alternatively, what they might well prefer is that Paul appear in the haughty arrogance and self-serving style of the rival apostles. Either way, Paul will have none of it: he is neither a wimp nor a triumphalist.

For his part, Paul does not want to arrive and find the Corinthians indulging in the sins of the spirit or in the sins of the flesh he lists. The first list is immediately linked with Paul's fear that the Corinthians may not be what he hopes they would be: "I fear that there may be quarreling, jealousy, outbursts of anger, factions, slander, gossip, arrogance and disorder" (12:20b). These sins were doubtless endemic at Corinth, as they are part and parcel of the party spirit that dominated their behavior (cf. 1 Cor 1:11-12,31; 3:3; 4:6; 8:1; 11:18; 14:33a); but they are also the sorts of sin that would be particularly prominent once the rival apostles took hold of the ministry there.

One of his reasons for writing, therefore, is to lay bare the kind of expectations each side had of the other, and to establish criteria for those expectations that would be in line with righteousness. The particular demonstration of righteousness Paul doubtless wants to see in this congregation is the serious effort to maintain the unity of the spirit through the bond of peace (cf. Eph 4:1-3).

But Paul has a third motive for writing:

3. To identify with his own wayward converts (12:21). It is remarkable that before listing some sins of the flesh that he earnestly hopes will not be present in the congregation when he arrives, Paul reflects another motive, or perhaps another face to the dominate motive of strengthening the believers he serves: "I am afraid that when I come again my God will humble me before you, and I will be grieved over many who have sinned earlier and have not repented of the impurity, sexual sin and debauchery in which they have indulged" (2 Cor 12:21). "Nothing brings a Christian teacher into the dust so much as the defection of those whom he has looked on as fruits of his labour and as his crown of rejoicing" (Beet).

This verse focuses on two principal themes. *First,* it contemplates the possibility that when Paul arrives the Corinthians will be awash in sexual sin. At first glance this is surprising, for sexual sin does not seem to play a major role in any part of 2 Corinthians.

The problem largely dissolves when we remember how prominent Paul's discussion of sexual sins was when he penned his first canonical epistle to the Corinthians. Not only did he have to deal with the shameful case of a church member sleeping with his stepmother (1 Cor 5:1-10) and with polarized opinions about sex, celibacy, marriage, and divorce (chap. 7), he also had to warn the Corinthian believers to "flee from sexual immorality" (6:18), explaining to them that freedom from the law does not sanction licentiousness (vv. 12-20). Christians are purchased people, bought at the terrible price of the Son of God's death; and therefore their conduct must honor him. The warning was particularly urgent in Corinth, where morals were so low that "a Corinthian girl" became a synonym for a harlot throughout the Mediterranean world, and where the professing believers still had such hazy notions of Christianity that they sometimes tried to domesticate theology to make it a servant of their lust.

Paul remembers the background of the Corinthians, and now fears that on his next trip to Corinth he will have to grieve again over those who sinned earlier (a reference to the situations he confronted in 1 Corinthians) and who have not repented of their sexual sin. Paul does not say that is the way it will be; indeed, if he were sure that such promiscuity were alive and well in Corinth, it is inconceivable he would not have confronted it more forcefully in this letter. But he fears it will be this way, for he recognizes that the kind of doctrinal, attitudinal, and spiritual sins he knows are rife at Corinth regularly provide the best soil for the sexual sins as well—especially in a city like Corinth, where sexual immorality was so common.

In short, Paul implicitly acknowledges a profound principle: the spiritual and doctrinal state of a church will sooner or later be reflected in the moral arena as well. This is not to say that if any *individual* Christian is immature or given to jealousy, factionalism, outbursts of anger, and the other sins listed, he or she will undoubtedly tumble into fornication. The connection is not anywhere near that close; there is no entailment at the individual level. But when a church or a denomination is characterized by such sins, it will not be long before it is also characterized by the grosser forms of immorality.

The reasons are pretty obvious. Not only do such professing believers, on average, lose the control of thought and motive that spiritual maturity brings, leaving sin far less restrained, but the church shot through with Corinthian problems cannot possibly exercise wise, firm, and loving discipline; and an *un*disciplined church sooner or later multiplies its sins. There may not be an entailment from, say, arrogance and factionalism to sexual immorality and debauchery at the individual level, as if each person guilty of the former must inevitably commit the latter; but there is certainly an entailment at the corporate level, both in terms of averages and in terms of general moral tone.

It follows that the low state of the sexual morality in many modern churches is likely an index of far deeper problems, the kinds of problems which Paul is seeking to handle in this epistle. Because he understands the connection, he fears that the repentance that seemed to alleviate the earlier promiscuity will prove false, and he will find triumphalism bedding down with licentiousness.

There is a *second* focus in this verse. Paul casts his fear in what at first appears to be a very strange phrasing: he fears that when he returns to Corinth again his God will humble him before the Corinthians. This humbling is clearly brought about by the need to deal with gross sin in a church that should have attained much more maturity by this point in its pilgrimage; yet Paul says he fears *God* will humble him, and that this humbling will be before the Corinthians. Why does he phrase his fear just this way?

What this very careful phrasing reflects is Paul's profound sense of responsibility for the churches he has founded and the Christians he has nurtured, coupled with a sustained belief that even in the apostle's failures God's sovereign purposes for good are being worked out. On the one hand, Paul sees the immaturity and sin of the Corinthians as in some sense his own failure. He clearly holds them responsible for their own sin, of course; for otherwise there would be little point in writing. But even so, he does not wash his hands of them, and say in effect, "I've done what I could. If you're going bad, so be it." Nor does he view with aloof equanimity the possibility he will need to impose apostolic discipline on the Corinthian church. Rather, although he is prepared to impose discipline, he treats the need to do so as a personal humiliation. He follows his own instruction: discipline may be necessary, but it must always be accompanied by tears (cf. 1 Cor 5:2). Not for him the haughty sternness of egocentric leaders who can with dry eyes and a high hand discipline members ensnared by sin. Paul is too much aware of the intertwining of responsibilities in the body of Christ. He cannot even distance himself entirely from their sin. He himself feels humbled in the face of it, just as a father feels humbled by his son's rebellion.

On the other hand, Paul understands that even in such pathetic and difficult situations, the bounds of God's sovereignty are not breached. In one sense therefore it is correct to say that if his fears are realized it will be God himself who is humbling the apostle, just as it was in some sense God himself who sent the thorn in the flesh (see discussion above on 2 Cor 12:7). Paul's perspective does not absolve the Corinthians of their responsibility, any more than it absolves Satan of his guilt in sending his messenger; but it does enable the apostle to carry on with full faith in the God who in all things works for the good of those who love him. Perhaps, Paul reasons, just as the thorn was sent to keep him from conceit, his humiliation in Corinth, should it take place, will advance his own maturity and witness as he carries in his body the death of Jesus (4:10), and preaches in his person as in his sermons the message of the cross (1 Cor 1:18). Moreover, as Barrett rightly notes, "That Paul *feared* this humiliation is no way inconsistent with his recognition in it of the hand of God; Jesus feared death (Mark xiv.33), and Paul prayed for the removal of the angel of Satan (xii.8)."

The Corinthians must understand, then, that one of Paul's motives is his driving desire to identify with his own wayward converts, while still discharging his responsibilities before God. That is not the least of his reasons for writing them in this manner; for if this work bears fruit, he will not be humiliated before his converts by their disgraceful conduct.

The rebuke is ended. Some of the worst failures of the Corinthians have been detailed, and contrasted with the apostles motives. It remains for Paul to offer a final word of warning, and to enunciate exactly what he is praying God will do in this painful situation.

Warning and Prayer
Aiming for Maturity

2 Corinthians 13:1-14

¹ This will be my third visit to you. "Every matter must be established by the testimony of two or three all numbers as witnesses." ² I already gave you a warning when I was with superscripts you the second time. I now repeat it while absent: On my return I will not spare those who sinned earlier or any of the others, ³ since you are demanding proof that Christ is speaking through me. He is not weak in dealing with you, but is powerful among you. ⁴ For to be sure, he was crucified in weakness, yet he lives by God's power. Likewise, we are weak in him, yet by God's power we will live with him to serve you.

⁵ Examine yourselves to see whether you are in the faith; test yourselves. Do you not realize that Christ Jesus is in you—unless, of course, you fail the test? ⁶ And I trust that you will discover that we have not failed the test. ⁷ Now we pray to God that you will not do anything wrong. Not that people will see that we have stood the test but that you will do what is right even though we may seem to have failed. ⁸ For we cannot do anything against the truth, but only for the truth. ⁹ We are glad whenever we are weak but you are strong; and our prayer is for your perfection. ¹⁰ This is why I write these things when I am absent, that when I come I may

not have to be harsh in my use of authority—the
authority the Lord gave me for building you up, not
for tearing you down.
   [11] Finally, brothers, good-by. Aim for perfection,
listen to my appeal, be of one mind, live in peace.
And the God of love and peace will be with you.
   [12] Greet one another with a holy kiss. [13] All the
saints send their greetings.
   [14] May the grace of the Lord Jesus Christ, and
the love of God, and the fellowship of the Holy
Spirit be with you all.

A. Warning (13:1-6)

1. Impending discipline in the third visit (13:1-3a). Paul's
first visit to Corinth had been for the purpose of planting a
church there (Acts 18:1-18; 1 Cor 4:15; 9:1). His second visit was
so painful both to him and to his converts that he resolved not to
visit them again for a while (2 Cor 1:23; 2:1). Now he contemplates
his third trip: "This will be my third visit to you," he writes,
resuming a point first introduced at 2 Cor 12:14.
   Paul's next sentence is a quotation from Deuteronomey 19:15:
Every "matter must be established by the testimony of two or
three witnesses." In the original context of the Pentateuch, this
was a judicial regulation to discourage arbitrary trials based on
the legal testimony of one biased witness who might be on some
personal vendetta. Appeal to the verse here certainly casts Paul's
third visit in a forensic light; but it is not entirely clear why Paul
quotes it. That he in some way relates the two or three witnesses
to the warning he gave when he was with them the second time
and to the prospect of the third visit is obvious; but the nature of
the relation is more obscure. After all, repeated trips and
warnings by one man are rather different from multiple witnesses.
   For this reason some have taken this quotation from Deuteronomy to be saying no more than that when Paul comes he will
be scrupulously fair: he will entertain no unsubstantiated charges.
This interpretation suits the context of Deuteronomy, but it is not
a very obvious way to take the words in the context of 2
Corinthians 13, primarily because it loses the link with the
second and third visit.

On the whole, therefore, it seems best to relate the two or three witnesses to the second and third visits, but to remember that Paul is not citing a proof text or an authorization text (there is no "as it is written"). Rather, Paul has used biblical phraseology to say, in effect, "I have given you due warning: on my next trip, if there is no improvement I will take decisive action."

That, at any rate, is what he goes on to say: "On my return I will not spare those who sinned earlier or any of the others, since you are demanding proof that Christ is speaking through me" (2 Cor 13:2b-3a). The words "I will not spare" in this context suggest Paul will be very stern in his use of apostolic authority if the conditions he fears are actually present. He hopes he will not have to be harsh in his use of authority (v. 10), but he points out elsewhere that he is prepared if necessary to use the whip (1 Cor 4:21).

Some scholars minimize the extent of Paul's authority, the snap in his whip. They hold he had no weapons of coercion whatever, nothing but the naked truth. The most Paul could do is was go to Corinth and speak the truth forcefully and courageously. If the Corinthians then chose to reject him, they would be rejecting the gospel; and in that case Paul could do nothing more.

This interpretation is too weak. Already in 1 Corinthians 5 Paul instructs the Corinthian church to hand over a particularly gross sinner to Satan "for the destruction of the flesh [not 'sinful nature' as in NIV!"]—i.e., Satan would inflict him with disease ultimately leading to death, unless repentance on the part of the sinner intervened, along with gracious restoration brought about by a forgiving God. This is not mere excommunication (although excommunication is normally the severest sanction the church may levy); and although the example in 1 Corinthians 5 is a *communal* decision fostered by Paul, the apostle is not restricted to communal approval. After all, in 1 Timothy 1:20 the apostle Paul, without the support or ratification of any church group, delivers Hymenaeus and Alexander to the same punishment.

What we must remember is that God hates sin, but doubly so when it proliferates among his own people. Judgment may sometimes delay a long time in coming; but that is not always a sign of mercy. It may be a sign of wrath, since the forbearance, rather sadly, may provide extra opportunity for storing up sins until the full measure of holy wrath is poured out. The sharpness of some of the discipline in the New Testament church is correspondingly a sign of mercy, for punishment long delayed loses all deterrence. Moreover, "the apostolic churches were not independent democratic communities vested with supreme authority over their own members. Paul could cast out of them whom he would" (Hodge).

The people who would be the principal target of Paul's discipline, granted that he finds the church in the shocking state he fears, are "those who sinned earlier or any of the others." He is referring first of all to those who might still be enmeshed in gross, sexual sin, and then secondarily to those in the church who are doing damage by other than sexual means (cf. 2 Cor 12:20).

Paul is particularly blunt in this threat because (he tells the Corinthians) "you are demanding proof that Christ is speaking through me" (2 Cor 13:3a). They were so sub-Christian in their thinking that Christlike gentleness and meekness meant little to them. They preferred manifestations of power, however exploitative and arbitrary they might be (11:20). Paul's gentleness they therefore misjudged as weakness, preferring the triumphalistic pushiness of the false apostles. Paul responds by saying that if it is power they want to see as the absolute criterion of genuine apostolicity, they may get more than they bargained for: he may be forced to display the power of the resurrected Christ, speaking through him in the thunderous tones of punishment, another version perhaps of the judgment meted out to Ananias and Sapphira (Acts 5:1-11).

2. Support for Paul's authority in the power of the resurrected Christ (13:3b-4). Paul now clarifies this last point. If it is Christ who is speaking through Paul, the Corinthians had better understand that, whatever they think of Paul, Christ himself "is not weak in dealing with you, but is powerful among you." In short, Paul is reminding his converts that their quarrel is ultimately with the glorified Christ, the risen Lord who has been exalted to the Father's right hand. Those who do damage to the church stand under the threat of divine retribution (1 Cor 3:17). Whatever weakness the Corinthians ascribe to Paul, they ought to recognize that behind Paul stands the omnipotent Christ, who will by no means permit the sins of the Corinthian church to run forever unchecked.

But as soon as he has said this, Paul recognizes that the Corinthians may misinterpret it. They may say to themselves, "You see? Christ himself is a figure of power! So why does Paul make so much of the meekness and gentleness of Christ when Paul himself is perfectly willing to draw attention to Christ's power when it suits him?" Paul must therefore demonstrate that the Lord Jesus Christ is the supreme example of both weakness and strength, and that these two virtues stand in a definite relation to each other.

"For to be sure," Paul writes, "he was crucified in (lit. 'out of') weakness, yet he lives by God's power." Christ has not always been characterized by displays of power. He lived and ministered in a spirit of meekness and gentleness, and he was crucified out of weakness. This peculiar way of phrasing things means something like "because of weakness." But Paul does not mean by this that Christ was crucified for no other reason than because he was weak, i.e., because he did not have the power to withstand his foes. Doubtless Paul was aware of Jesus' claim, even in Gethsemane, that he had at his disposal legions of angels (Matt 26:53; cf. John 10:18). Christ was never so weak he was forced to death as is a martyr. What Paul means is that Christ lay down his life "out of" the context of weakness, i.e., because weakness was what he had chosen in his determination to do the Father's will. He was crucified because of weakness in the sense that all the benefits that flow to us from his grace gush forth out of the context of his own self-denial, the just dying for the unjust to bring us to God.

Christ was crucified out of weakness; yet, Paul goes on to insist, "he lives by God's power." In other words, "the cross does not exhaust Christ's relation to sin; He passed from the cross to the throne, and when He comes again it is as Judge" (Denney). Paul himself does not here lay out quite so much detail; but his point is similar. Jesus' self-adopted weakness, supremely displayed in his crucifixion, is not the last word: God raised him from the dead. Here is a shattering manifestation of power; and this is as characteristic of Jesus as the weakness of the cross. The cross and the resurrection go together; Jesus displays both weakness and power.

But in this manifestation of dual virtues, Christ stands as a model for Christians; and if for Christians, then supremely for

Christian apostles. That is the conclusion Paul draws; for once he has described Christ's display of both weakness and power, he writes, "Likewise, we are weak in him, yet by God's power we will live with him to serve you" (2 Cor 13:4b). Paul means that his own experience will mirror Christ's (cf. 4:10). Like all other believers, the apostle Paul lives this side of death; and therefore one principal sign of Christian existence will be "the same kind of vulnerability that Christ himself chose to adopt" (Barrett). Powerful life is primarily the prospect of the future; for although Christ has been raised from the dead as the firstfruits of believers, the believers themselves do not experience the same power to a similar degree until Christ returns (1 Cor 15:20-28). Some of that resurrection power is operative in believers now to make us holy (e.g., Eph 1:19-20; 3:16-17); and in the apostle Paul, some of that same resurrection power has been granted to enable him to handle the Corinthian situation. In Paul's weakness, God's power will be perfectly displayed "to serve you," for the Corinthians' benefit (even if discipline is not usually perceived as a benefit at the time by those who undergo it, Heb 12:5-13).

Paul's main points are clear. On his prospective third trip, he threatens to bring stern discipline if that is necessary (2 Cor 13:1-3a); and the display of power such discipline presupposes will be supported by nothing less than the power of the resurrected Christ. This inevitably leads to a further warning: if judgment is so impending, then the Corinthians ought to examine themselves to ward off possible destruction.

3. Self-test for the Corinthians (13:5). The Corinthian believers, confident of their own wisdom, had been blissfully testing Paul and other claimants to apostleship; but they should have been testing themselves. "Examine yourselves to see whether you are in the faith," Paul writes; "test yourselves" (2 Cor 13:5a). The word "yourselves" is emphatic in position: yourselves, as opposed to everybody else. In an earlier letter Paul told them to "stand firm in the faith" (1 Cor 16:13); now he tells them to examine themselves to see if they are "in the faith." In both instances "in the faith" means "in the Christian faith," i.e., in the Christian religion, designated "faith" by Paul because it is the God-revealed religion which, from the human perspective, is characterized by faith.

Now if the Corinthians are truly Christians, they will realize that Christ Jesus is in them—unless, of course, they fail the test. If Christ Jesus is in them, then they, like Paul, should hunger to know something of Christ's meekness and gentleness, something of his weakness. Like Paul, they will pursue not only the power of his resurrection but also "the fellowship of sharing in his sufferings, becoming like him in his death" (Phil 3:10). That is what they must inevitably come to recognize—unless of course they fail the test.

Paul has wisely placed the Corinthians in a cleft stick. Since in his metaphor they administer the test to themselves, they are unlikely to fail themselves. The logic of Paul's entire presentation, however, demands that if they "pass" themselves, they must pursue the crucified Christ as diligently as they pursue the exalted Christ. The only alternative is that they fail the test.

That Paul should encourage believers to indulge in the introspection of self-examination has raised many questions in the minds of some readers. In the magisterial Reformation, so much emphasis was placed on the fact that salvation was by grace, through faith alone, that many reformers equated saving faith with assurance. If a believer lacks assurance, it was argued, it is because he or she lacks truly saving faith. Calvin himself draws a false negative inference from this text, saying that Paul "declares that those who doubt their possession of Christ and their membership in His Body are reprobates"—which of course does not follow from the text.

The truth is that doubt regarding one's status before the sovereign Lord can stem from many different causes. If doubt springs from uncertainty regarding the sufficiency of Christ's cross-work, then the doubting believer must be led back to the many passages that attest its perfection. But if doubt springs from suppressed sin, the proper course for removal of the doubt is repentance of the sin, confession, and, where possible, restitution. Similarly, if a believer is very confident he is accepted in the beloved and is written in the Lamb's book of life, not because he feels morally superior, but because he thoughtfully joins the Lord's people in singing

> Nothing in my hands I bring
> Only to Thy cross I cling.

—then self-examination is superfluous. If, however, this alleged believer is puffed up with unrestrained self-importance, unqualified self-love, moral laxness or major doctrinal deviation, then the apostle John (to go no farther) has a set of three tests to impose (1 John): doctrinal commitment, love for the brothers, and moral obedience to Christ Jesus. If someone fails any one of these tests, John declares that person is no Christian at all (e.g., 1 John 2:1-9). At this point the emphasis of the reformers is seen to be a trifle simplistic; for in the appropriate situations, the Scriptures focus on subjective grounds of assurance (i.e., transformed lives), just as in other contexts they focus on the objective ground (the cross-work of Christ).

In short, when a person is broken in spirit and contrite before the God of all justice, grace comes and pronounces absolution and grants confidence. But when a person is haughty and arrogant, the product of well-cultivated triumphalism, unconscious of grace or of any need for it, then grace flees and a stern apostle warns, "Examine yourselves to see whether you are in the faith; test yourselves."

There are millions of professing believers in North America today (to say nothing of elsewhere) who at some point entered into a shallow commitment to Christianity, but who, if pushed, would be forced to admit they do not love holiness, do not pray, do not hate sin, do not walk humbly with God. They stand in the same danger as the Corinthians; and Paul's warning applies to them no less than to the Corinthian readers of this epistle.

4. Entailment of passing the test (13:6). Paul's next step at first sight seems out of context: he switches from talking about the Corinthians' passing or failing, to his own passing of the test. Then suddenly what Paul is up to becomes clear, and we realize he takes a brilliant step when he writes, "And I trust that you will discover that we have not failed the test."

Paul's point is that if the Corinthians, as a result of their self-examination, decide that they are true believers, then there is an unavoidable entailment: the man who led them to their first steps of faith and their initial experiences of grace cannot be quite as useless as some of them have been suggesting. There must be some merit at least to his claims to apostolicity: i.e., Paul passes the test they have erected.

The irony is rich. If the Corinthians declare they have failed the test, then doubtless Paul will be humiliated (cf. 2 Cor 12:21); but in that case the Corinthians are in no position to point the finger at anyone. If on the other hand, they feel they have passed the test, then since Paul did all the initial evangelization among them he is the last person they are in a position to condemn.

Clearly this is not a principle that is universally applicable. For instance, not every evangelist is laying claims to apostolic powers; and in some cases the evangelist himself might have turned renegade in the interim between his evangelization of a particular group and the application of the test. Nor is this exactly the same as saying that success validates all credentials. The argument works well in this context because of the peculiar nature of the charges leveled against Paul by the Corinthian church.

The warning is over. Paul now turns to the prayer he constantly offers to God for the Corinthians.

B.   Prayer (13:7-9)

1. Its object (13:7a). "Now we pray to God that you will not do anything wrong." Paul might have been spending time praying for his personal apostolic vindication, or at least that the Corinthians might come to their senses; but his grasp of priorities does not fail. He prays that in this present confrontation the Corinthian church might do no wrong, i.e., that they will be preserved and restrained from sin. "This is the most desirable thing we can ask God, both for ourselves and for our friends, that we and they may do no evil; and it is most needful, that we often pray to God for the grace to keep us, because without that we cannot keep ourselves. We are more concerned to pray that we may not *do* evil, than that we may not *suffer* evil" (Henry).

2. Its motive (13:7b). Paul knows his Corinthians. He is all too aware that they have a penchant for twisting his argument to mean that he is fawning up to them, trying to honey up to their good graces again (cf. 3:1; 5:12; 12:19). Anticipating that even at this late stage in the argument some of the believers in Corinth might twist his reference to passing the test to mean he is still after some shoddy bit of personal gain, Paul insists not only that his central prayer in these circumstances is that the Corinthian believers may do no wrong, but that he is able to utter such a prayer with complete, personal disinterest: "Not that people will see that we have stood the test but that you will do what is right even though we may seem to have failed."

Paul's argument is profoundly humbling. His prayer is that the Corinthians might do no wrong; and in this context, the wrong they might do is to continue with their triumphalism and its evil entailments (cf. 2 Cor 12:20-21), including the failure to take appropriate action against the intruding false apostles (cf. 10:1-2,6). If the Corinthians do the right thing, not only will they be pleasing God, but they will avoid the display of apostolic severity and power (cf. 13:2,10). Of course, in that case Paul might once again appear weak to them: he promised to come in power, they might say, but once again he shows up with what he calls the meekness and gentleness of Christ.

No matter: "It would be better for the Corinthians to do what they knew to be good and right, even if this were to place Paul seemingly in the wrong, than that they should do something wrong" (Harris). It is doubtful if Paul is very sanguine about the outcome; but whatever the personal price, he is willing to pay it if only their own conduct is right before God and man.

Here is the heart of a true apostle, a Christian so steeped in radical discipleship and firm self-discipline that his every care is for the people he serves, not for his own reputation. He is no hireling, but a true under-shepherd, willing to be counted a failure, a sinner, even a counterfeit, if only the people he serves may be lifted up in their faith. Paul is the perfect antithesis to triumphalistic leadership.

3. Its assurance (13:8). Paul's next words are so aphoristic they are a little difficult to understand: "For we cannot do anything against the truth, but only for the truth." One way of taking it appears to be as a statement reflecting Paul's determination: i.e., the "cannot" is not an ontological impossibility, but Pauline assurance of what he would not do under any circumstance. He cannot do anything against the truth, even if it means he himself is misunderstood by his converts; he can only act for the truth, i.e., in line with the gospel of God and all that entails in the lives of believers.

Alternatively, it is just possible Paul means that he cannot do anything against the gospel, where the truth already exists. He cannot use his apostolic authority to provide a display of powerful confrontation and discipline in a situation where the truth already has free course in the lives of the people, for that would be to undermine the truth. He can use his apostolic powers of discipline only for the truth, i.e., where gospel purity is lacking and needs to be restored. This latter interpretation admirably fits the context of this passage. It suggests once again that the display of apostolic power the Corinthians so much want to see is something Paul would use only as a last resort to restore the truth. His normal approach is to avoid such power confrontations. The aphorism thereby provides assurance that Paul's prayer for the Corinthians is backed up by the assurance of a distinctively Christian mix of apostolic weakness and strength.

4. Its aim (13:9). Paul's point now comes clear, as he overtly returns to the heart of his prayer: "We are glad whenever we are weak but you are strong; and our prayer is for your perfection." Paul's constant, burning prayer is for the Corinthians' perfection, i.e., their restoration to Christian values, their achievement of some degree of real maturity, their abandonment of the false gospel, their rejection of false apostles, their pursuit of Christian character. Nothing pleases Paul more than to see his converts mature, strong, and robust in their faith. He is glad, he says, when they are strong. If this means he appears weak, i.e., lacking in displays of power, he is still glad. He has no desire to set up scenes where he may use his apostolic authority to build a kind of personal aura. He would much rather leave his apostolic arsenal at home, and watch his converts grow to the full maturity that does not need the constant external discipline and regulation of an apostle.

There is a very humbling model for all true Christian leadership in Paul's relationship with the Corinthians. Pressed to the limit, his attitude is not at all retaliatory and cheap. He still desires above all the spiritual well-being of his converts. Of no interest to him at all are questions of personal gain, financial reward, security, promotion, or personal reputation. His energies are focused on bringing his converts to maturity, restoration, perfection. If along the way this entails further steps of self-abasement, he is not perturbed by the prospect. What upsets him far more is the possible need for confrontation, for that would suggest there are all too many serious sins in the congregation. In no respect does Paul more closely resemble the Master he loves and serves than in his attitude to the church of which he is an apostle. May God raise up a generation of like-minded spiritual leaders.

C. Paul's Balanced Purpose in Writing (13:10)

"This is why I write these things when I am absent, that when I come I may not have to be harsh in my use of authority— the authority the Lord gave me for building you up, not for tearing you down." In this sentence Paul tells his readers at least part of the purpose in his writing; but in some respects the verse also serves as a summary of 2 Corinthians 10-13. Paul has been charged with writing weighty letters while absent, yet proving weak when he shows up personally on the scene. In one sense the charge is justified; but Paul says the reason why he writes these things, during his absence from the Corinthians is so that when he actually arrives he will not have to be harsh in his use of the apostolic authority entrusted to him. If the letter does its proper work, there will be repentance and obedience to the gospel in Corinth, and Paul will not be forced to display the stern power of discipline with which the Corinthian believers are otherwise threatened.

Thus Paul simultaneously hopes for good results, and issues a final warning in case his hopes are dashed. He recognizes that the overarching purpose of God in entrusting authority to him is to build the church; yet he knows that sometimes a necessary if painful intermediate step is to tear down faulty construction (cf. also 2 Cor 10:8). However reluctant the apostle is to use his power in so destructive a fashion, he quietly reminds the church, one more time, that he is prepared to take such steps if his letter does not succeed in purifying the church in advance of his arrival.

It is important to recognize the sweep and independence of the apostolic authority presupposed by such a warning. Although Paul sees that in certain respects the evidence of his apostolic authority is the Corinthian church itself, along with other churches he has established, his authority is in no way dependent on those churches. If the Corinthian church should prove largely false, he feels free to destroy the work and remove the rot, in the hope of building something better. That is not his preference: he prefers to devote his energies to edification, not to discipline. But he is aware of the authority given to him to accomplish either task. Which one he will have to perform in this case now depends very much on the Corinthians themselves.

D. Final Greetings (13:11-14).

In these final lines, 2 Corinthians 13:11 still casts a backward glance at the rest of the epistle, whereas the remaining verses might well be found at the end of any of Paul's letters. Paul announces the end of his missive with a cautious "Finally, brothers, good-by." Then, as if he is still burdened for his readers and cannot let them go without offering one more brief word of exhortation, he provides four brief injunctions.

The *first* is, "Aim for perfection" (the word used is cognate with the "perfection" mentioned in 2 Cor 13:9). There he prayed for the Corinthians' perfection; here he exhorts them to it. In both instances he is after the same thing: Christian maturity. In the context of the entire epistle, this injunction means, in practical terms, that the Corinthians must receive Paul's delegates with Christian hospitality, abandon any lingering idolatry (6:14-7:1), continue preparing a generous contribution for the relief of the poor believers in Jerusalem, and, in the light of the last four chapters, abandon triumphalism and one-upmanship while instituting discipline in the church.

The *second* injunction is, "Listen to my appeal." This too forces the readers—whether the Corinthians or ourselves—to review the epistle. More, it makes the exhortation to aim for perfection a question of obedience to apostolic appeal and exhortation, not an optional extra.

"Be of one mind," the *third* injunction, probably means more than "get along with one another." Rather, Paul wants the members of the Corinthian church so to work through their differences of opinions, bringing them to the test of the apostolic gospel, that they will become of one mind. As he writes to them elsewhere, "I appeal to you, brothers, in the name of our Lord Jesus Christ, that all of you agree with one another so that there may be no divisions among you and that you may be perfectly united in mind and thought" (1 Cor 1:10). Modern evangelicals who share a common allegiance to the Scriptures would do well to foster this sort of attempt to come to one mind and thought as to what the Scriptures mean. Too many of us are so threatened by our fellow believers or are so bound up with our denominational distinctives, that we are afraid to be reformed by the Word of God or too proud to be corrected by those with whom we disagree. The apostle expects us to work at the business of being of one mind.

Fourth, Paul tells the Corinthians to "live in peace." One-upmanship and triumphalism invariably breed polarization, jealousy, factions, slander. If the Corinthian believers repent of the sins at the core of their rebellion, they will overcome some of the entailments. The injunction to live in peace focuses on those entailments and reflects the high priority the Bible places on the demonstration of unity and peace among God's people (e.g., Eph 4:1-3).

To these four injunctions Paul appends a blessing: "And the God of love and peace will be with you" (2 Cor 13:11). This could be taken in one of two ways. It might mean that God, the source of love and peace, will provide his own resources of these virtues to empower the Corinthians to obey the injunctions. The expression "the God of love and peace" in that case means that God is the giver of love and peace. Alternatively, and perhaps somewhat better in this context, love and peace may be seen less as God's gifts than as God's characteristics (cf. Rom 5:8; 1 Cor 14:33). In that case the promise of the presence of the God of love and peace is contingent upon obedience to the injunctions. If the Corinthians aim for perfection, listen to Paul's appeal, learn to be of one mind and live in peace; they will find that the God of love and peace is with them. Otherwise, they will discover that the same God is the one who empowers the apostle Paul to bring stern discipline to the wayward people of God.

Paul winds up with some standard salutations that he invests with Christian overtones. The kiss was a common form of greeting in the Mediterranean world, and still is in many places. But Paul tells the Corinthians to greet one another with a "holy kiss," not because he is suggesting that kisses by non-Christians are "unholy," but because the fellowship and love that the kiss of greeting ought to reflect in the Christian community are holy (cf. also Rom 16:16; 1 Cor 16:20). It goes beyond the evidence to label the holy kiss a cultic act, as if it belonged to a set liturgy; but at its best it ought to reflect unity of mind coupled with love and peace in the Christian assembly.

At the same time the Corinthians need to be reminded they are not the only Christians in the world. The sentence "All the saints send their greetings" (2 Cor 13:13)—presumably all the believers in the area from which Paul writes, the Christians in one of the Macedonian churches such as Philippi, Thessalonica, or Berea—is therefore more than courtesy: it is a healthy reminder to all believers from the Corinthians on to see themselves as part, but only part, of the entire body of Christ. Such a sense of unity should prove both exhilarating and sobering. It should afford us a vision of the scope of God's redemptive operation, yet permit us to see our local group of believers is not the center of the entire church. The Corinthian way was to trivialize the gospel and the church, while magnifying believers. God's way is to display the grandeur of the church, while humbling believers.

And so we arrive at the final benediction: "May the grace of the Lord Jesus Christ, and the love of God, and the fellowship of the Holy Spirit be with you all" (2 Cor 13:14). The order of the persons of the Godhead—Son, Father, Holy Spirit instead of the more usual Father, Son, Holy Spirit—may owe something to the enormous emphasis on self-sacrifice and self-abasement in these chapters (cf. 8:9), since those virtues were so magnificently manifested by Christ. The grace shown by Christ condemns our self-centeredness and triumphalism, the love of God demonstrated by Christ's grace banishes our jealousy and factionalism, and the fellowship the Holy Spirit creates among us renders ridiculous the petty one-upmanship of minds mired in self.

E. Aftermath

Did these chapters turn the situation in Corinth around? We do not know for certain. Elsewhere, a group of churches or church leaders abandoned Paul (cf. 2 Tim 1:15), despite his warning about the impending defection (Acts 20:29-31). But in this case, there are small bits of evidence to suggest that the Corinthians responded positively to Paul's moving epistle and obeyed his injunctions. The most important evidence springs from the fact that when the threatened third visit actually took place (cf. vv. 2, 3), Paul found time to write his Epistle to the Romans. That letter betrays some anxiety about the future (15:30-31), but none about the present. Moreover, in light of his remarks in 2 Corinthians 10:15-16a, Paul would not have been planning at that time to travel on to Spain (Rom 15:24-28) if the Corinthian situation were still unresolved. The fact that the Corinthians collected their share of the funds Paul was gathering for the believers in Jerusalem (Rom 15:26, 27) presupposes, to say the least, that there was no final rupture between the apostle and the Corinthians.

Yet for our purposes, the most important question we may ask concerns what effect this book will have in our own lives and congregations. The Word of God Written by the apostle Paul does not have its most potent effect on our lives when we ask antiquarian questions about the way it has touched others, but when we wholeheartedly obey it.